OPEN-KITCHEN RESTAURANT

Edited by Laura Vulto

DESIGN MEDIA PUBLISHING LIMITED

Contents

Preface:
Design Is Merged

Design Is Merged

The trend of integrating the kitchen into the restaurant and making it a visible element, started in the beginning of the year 2000. A new food culture emerged which was triggered by the new public interest in gastronomy and the need to reconnect with preparing food. This together with the emerging questions regarding the origin of food, made us rethink the restaurant design as we knew it.

Chefs started branding themselves while the story behind the food became essential. A restaurant wasn't just a place anymore where you could satisfy your desire for good food and social interaction; it became a place where you are entertained and involved as a spectator in the process of preparing the food.

La Place, the famous Dutch restaurant concept, was one of the precursors of this trend in The Netherlands. They introduced an accommodating live cooking concept and showed that there was a need for a more flexible way of eating. Influenced by the Asian food culture where you can eat whatever, whenever and wherever, the concept turned out to be a big hit appealing to a large audience.

This trend also touched down in New York in places such as the Gramercy Tavern, an established example of the evolution of the traditional restaurant lay out to todays design. Other than what you might expect, the best seats in this restaurant are the ones at the bar; it's the interaction with the kitchen what makes these seats so popular. They are closest to the kitchen allowing the guest to be part of the cooking experience. It creates a relationship between the chef and his audience, making them feel special.

To us, Amsterdam-based interior design firm D/DOCK, this is a key factor when we design a restaurant; we want to make people feel special and appreciated by considering them as guests and not as customers. By creating an inviting environment where the guest is in charge and interaction arises between the different users, the open kitchen becomes the island of the restaurant. It is the place where all people gather around, just like your own cooking island in your kitchen back at home.

Fitch & Shui, one of our latest hospitality concepts in Amsterdam, is such a restaurant. Finger food, pizza and other small bites are prepared at the 20-meter long bar and directly served to the guest sitting there. By doing so, the bar becomes the extension of the kitchen making it the social island of the restaurant.

Photography: Render Fitch &Shui: D/DOCK

Photography: Render Fitch &Shui: D/DOCK

Another example that breaks with all traditional rules of restaurant design is Restaurant Vandaag Amsterdam. Paying by the hour, it is not about how much you eat; it is about how long you are staying. The live cooking stations and the variety of different cuisines and products makes this restaurant feel like a market place where you can shop around for food. After having selected all the ingredients, the chef behind the cooking station will prepare your dish on the spot. This is where the magic happens by turning cooking into entertainment.

Photography: Alan Jensen

Photography: Foppe Peter Schut

The ultimate food experience is the cooking school we designed for BSH Huishoudapparaten at the Amsterdam area, the headquarters of home appliance brands Bosch, Siemens, Gaggenau, Neff and Constructa. Being guided by a professional chef you prepare your own dish and eat it afterwards, which transforms the kitchen into your own restaurant. You become part of the environment by being the chef and the guest at the same time.

To D/DOCK, a good restaurant design is all about creating the ultimate experience. The kitchen, the beating heart of a restaurant, is the primary tool to do so. Creating an open kitchen connects the most important element of a restaurant with its audience, making a restaurant alive and transparent.

D/DOCK
NieuweSpiegelstraat 36
1017 DG Amsterdam
The Netherlands

www.ddock.com
Twitter @DDockDesign
Facebook D/DOCK

Chapter 1 :
Brief Introduction of Open Kitchens

As interior design goes, the open kitchen is a relative youngster. It is a modern idea, and with it come challenges. In the past, restaurant customers may have preferred food to magically appear out from behind closed doors, with no indication whatsoever about how the sausage is made – figuratively or literally. After years of hearing Big Food and fast food horror stories that'll turn stomach, however, the prototypical modern diner seems to want transparency rather than mystery. (See Figure 1.1, 1.2)

1.1 Definition and Forms of Open Kitchens

1.1.1 Definition
In home space design, an open kitchen refers to the open cooking-dining space that integrates dining table and kitchen through skillful use of space.

In commercial space, an open kitchen refers to commercial kitchen in public space which takes pipelined gas, natural gas or bottled gas as

Figure 1.1,1.2: Open kitchen in the restaurant to show the cooking process in front of diners

fuel and non-load transparent component such as tempered glass as partitions or without any partitions to dining area.

1.1.2 Forms (See Figure 1.3, 1.4, 1.5, 1.6)
According to operation requirements, open kitchens can be divided into two forms: full-open kitchen and semi-open kitchen. Full-open kitchen joins kitchen and dining area together to form a whole space. Some restaurants also keep the cooking area closed and preparation area open. The openings of connections between kitchen and other areas vary in size according to design requirements. The opening for pass-through is smaller while the opening for viewing is larger without partitions or fireproof cut-off. According to different show areas, full-open kitchens try to show cooking, washing and sterilisation processes show the diners fully. The kitchen is combined with the front dining area to delete pass-through step and reduce the dish-passing time from kitchen to diners. Meanwhile, the supervision of diners reinforces their interactions. As an

Figure 1.3,1.4,1.5,1.6: Open kitchens in restaurants in different forms

1.5

1.6

innovative management and operation mode, full-open kitchen proposes higher requirement in planning and design.

Semi-open kitchen takes whole-face or large area of non-load transparent material as partition, which means the division material between kitchen and restaurant is not fireproofing. As an example of semi-open kitchen, cooking station uses transparent partition (often a sheet of glass) to connect kitchen and restaurant. The rough processing and cooked food are finished in back of house. Only the food and final step of cooking are shown in front of diners. The diners could enjoy the cooking show freely. This semi-open mode assures diners in the term of sanitation. However, the diners cannot smell the dishes because of the glass partition, which also widens the distance between kitchen and diners. With simple kitchen equipment, semi-open kitchen requires a spacious, bright and aesthetic design. The compounding equipments include show counters and showcases.

1.2 Origin and Development of Open Kitchens

Starting in the 1980s, the perfection of the extractor hood allowed an open kitchen again, integrated more or less with the living room without causing the whole apartment or house to smell. Before that, only a few earlier experiments, typically in newly built upper-middle-class family homes, had open kitchens. Examples are Frank Lloyd Wright's House Willey (1934) and House Jacobs (1936). Both had open kitchens, with high ceilings (up to the roof) and were aired by skylights. The extractor hood made it possible to build open kitchens in apartments, too, where both high ceilings and skylights were not possible.

The re-integration of the kitchen and the living area went hand in hand with a change in the perception of cooking: increasingly, cooking was seen as a creative and sometimes social act instead of work. And there was a rejection by younger home-owners of the standard suburban model of separate kitchens and dining rooms found in most 1900-1950 houses. Many families also appreciated the trend towards open kitchens, as it made it easier for the parents to supervise the children while cooking and clear up spills. The enhanced status of cooking also made the kitchen a prestige object for showing off one's wealth or cooking professionalism. Some architects have capitalised on this "object" aspect of the kitchen by designing freestanding "kitchen objects".

Another reason for the trend back to open kitchens (and a foundation of the "kitchen object" philosophy) is changes in how food is prepared. Whereas prior to the 1950s most cooking started out with raw ingredients and a meal had to be prepared from scratch, the advent of frozen meals and pre-prepared convenience food changed the cooking habits of many people, who consequently used the kitchen less and less. For others, who followed the "cooking as a social act" trend, the open kitchen had the advantage that they could be with their guests while cooking, and for the "creative cooks" it might even become a stage for their cooking performance. The "Trophy Kitchen" is highly equipped with very expensive and sophisticated appliances which are used primarily to impress visitors and to project social status, rather than for actual cooking.

Street hawkers in Southeast Asia were the first breed of show kitchens. This was more of a necessity rather than for "show" sake. Japanese teppan-yaki outlets have been utilising this concept for decades. Now, show kitchens are sprouting all over hotels and restaurants in Asia Pacific. In Hong Kong, this uniquely modern phenomenon of "Open Kitchen" concept has been gaining popularity. The kitchen, once literally and figuratively the "back of house", has stepped into the forefront. Restaurateurs are becoming quick to allow roaming eyes into "back of house" areas. The kitchen has taken on a prominent role in providing entertainment, leading the way for "Show Kitchens" and "Open Kitchens".

1.2.1 Open Kitchens in Houses
A simple and spacious open kitchen design will be inevitably favourable to modern people when choosing commercial housing or selecting home decoration. Although with troubles of cooking fumes, many urbanites

who pursue comfortable sensations and fashion still look forward to open kitchens.

Open plan living spaces have become very popular in recent years as domestic dwellings have become smaller. Creating one large room out of 2 or 3 smaller rooms makes the living space feel larger and more contemporary.

This is an undertaking most often taken up by those whose kids have grown up and left home, or those with disposable income enough to sustain this kind of a change in the layout of their home. Having an open plan kitchen gives your home a flow it otherwise wouldn't have, with room enough for walking space as well as living space and a feel of openness and easy-access to the kitchen area.

A sense of togetherness is achieved, with the ordinarily separate rooms in the house consolidated into a more centralised living space, making the home less compartmentalised. This has its obvious advantages.

The kitchen as wide-open continuation of the living space (rather than tucked-away scullery) brings its own set of questions, such as clear and sensible spatial geometry, definition of function, sufficient wall space for big appliances, and lighting. "The hardest part is visibility. It becomes more than just working space, because everything is on stage and exposed," says Tom Shafer, a principal of Grunsfeld Shafer Architects in Chicago. For a couple who wanted to stay put in the 1950s ranch house they had come to love over many years, Shafer did an extensive remodel, designing the entire house – including the open kitchen – by following the home's existing lines. "They wanted to keep their memories and use the house with the next generation, their married children and grandchildren," Shafer says.

1.2.2 Open Kitchens in Restaurants (See Figure 1.7, 1.8, 1.9, 1.10)
Nowadays, open kitchens are not only popular in houses, many upscale western restaurants and star-rating hotels also arrange them in dining

area to create an open cooking concept and sense. The extensive use of open kitchens has become an overwhelming catering trend. Open kitchens are blended into upscale culinary culture in a modern, fashion, aesthetic and friendly posture and play a significant role.

Figure 1.7,1.8,1.9,1.10: Chefs work in the open kitchen

For diners, open kitchens enable them to view the flow of work of kitchens and unique techniques from chefs. A kitchens is divided into two areas: closed kitchen and open kitchen. The closed kitchen is mainly used for rough processing and chopping and assembling of materials for barbecue dishes and cooking of other dishes, while the open kitchen is responsible of final cooking and final plate of barbecue dishes. This makes cooking a scene feeling. The popularity of cooking show attributes to open kitchen's natures of freedom, freshness and quick upgrade.

For maximum transparency, restaurants ranging from fast-casual superstar Chipotle, to indie eateries favored by foodies, to massive fast-food chains like Domino's are all turning to the open kitchen.

The open kitchen trend seems to have been born in big cities such as New York, where chefs cooked within view of diners largely due to space constraints. Getting in the habit of watching chefs do their thing on TV has obviously boosted the fascination with what goes on in restaurant kitchens. As diners grew obsessed with celebrity chefs and the creative ways fresh and exotic ingredients were being combined, consumers increasingly came to view the flames and steam and clattering in the kitchen as part of the "show" of dining out.

The open kitchen trend trickled down to the growing fast casual market, most obviously with the wildly successful Chipotle chain. The "Chipotle Experience," as it's called, is deeply rooted in transparency, with all the ingredients of burritos, bowls, tacos, and salads "laid out in front so one can choose the perfect combination to make perfect meal." All of the chopping and assembling of food takes place in full view of customers (behind glass), purposefully so. Here's part of Chipotle's explanation for why the open kitchen design is so important: the sounds, the smells, and the sights of cooking can really help work up an appetite. Unfortunately in a lot of restaurants the "cooking" they do is more like putting together a science experiment. To that end, each Chipotle is designed with a kitchen that's open to the entire restaurant.

QSR Magazine named "Transparency" one of the biggest quick service restaurant trends, anticipating that more restaurants will "follow the trend of open kitchens as a sign to customers that they have nothing to hide." By now, the open kitchen has spread to smaller cities such as Milwaukee. "I do think Milwaukee is catching up to a more national trend," said one chef in the city. "Thanks to celebrity chefs and good food, the dining public wants to see what's going on. Also chefs, me included, are proud of what we do and like to showcase our habitat."

"Open Kitchen of Flame Cooking" at Towngas Avenue (See Figure 1.11)
"Open Kitchen of Flame Cooking" in Towngas Avenue is more than the

expansion of the kitchen function. It performs a dual function of production and entertainment. Not only they can enjoy different cuisine, premium beverages and freshly baked snacks prepared by "Flame Cooking", but also enjoy the entertainment produced by "Flame cooking". The "Show Kitchen" provides suspense and action for the diners, through the flashes of fire, the sounds of food sizzling, and the chef's chopping and cooking skills. Diners can have a unique dining-out experience provided by this "Open Kitchen of Flame Cooking".

Generally speaking, the open kitchen is still a concept. The degree of opening needs to be decided by actual requirements. Of course, people could also achieve open kitchen concept in their unique methods.

1.10

1.11

Figure 1.11: Layout plan of Towngas Avenue in Causeway Bay

Chapter 2 :
Design Principles

2.1 Designing Process

2.2 Factors to Be Considered

"Open kitchens (display kitchen, show kitchen or presentation kitchen) are rapidly gaining prominence, not only because they offer a way to express the concept of a restaurant, but they also attract guests' interest towards the process of cooking", Praveen K Singh once pointed out.

Often the idea of an open kitchen or display kitchen is categorised as a trend in kitchen design. In fact, it is a trend in restaurant concepts. And by "restaurants", it means almost every location where customers gather to select and enjoy food; therefore traditional restaurants, food courts, canteens at institutions and healthcare dining facilities for ambulatory patients, staff, visitors and guests are all included in the definition.

Says M Ram Vittal Rao, hotel consultant, who has designed the largest number of interactive display kitchens in the country, "I can certainly say that an enormous proportion of the kitchens we craft today include an open or display area. In most cases, a major part of the kitchen is in view of ordering and dining customers. 60 to 80 percent of the food which is in the process of preparation or at least in the final stages occurs in full view of customers, so as to reinforce freshness and to enhance customers' appetites."

The design of an open kitchen is invovled with several principles and amount of factors need to be considered. (See Figure 2.1, 2.2)

Figure 2.1,2.2: Food are prepared in front of diners

2.1 Designing Process

It remains a fact that the design process has an established sequence of events that must be completed for the best results. Each stage in the process builds on work completed in the previous stages – it is a cumulative effort.

Master planning is the first step in the process, where one establishes what the project should consist of, or if it should exist at all. The main objectives of this phase are justification of the project and exploration of potential design solutions

Programming
Once one has determined that the project is at least worth exploring, a narrative should be developed that will describe the scope of the project as well as its various "components", such as the individual areas within a single facility, or facilities that comprise a greater complex. This narrative will often include required adjacencies (areas that must be located next to each other), desired sizing, and any special requirements or considerations. The programme communicates the owner's desires and requirements to the design team in written form.

Concept Design
This is often the first time that the effort includes any form of graphic communication. The conceptual design is the first attempt to translate the written programme into graphic form. It will typically consist of "bubble diagrams", which identify the anticipated location and size of each area in the program. It may also consist of renderings that highlight the exterior, entry, or other key design elements of the project.

Schematic Design
This phase in the design process builds on the concept phase through the development of block/schematic drawings, geared to identify elements such as walls, counters, and key pieces of furniture or equipment. These drawings focus on defining the footprint of the space, but do not contain a

great deal of detail within these "blocks".

Design Development
At the end of this stage, the general floor plan is typically locked in and the detail within each space must be defined and developed. While a restaurant's locations and dimensions might have been identified in the Schematic Phase, it is in Design Development where the individual pieces of equipment are selected and incorporated into the design. At the end of this phase, it should be expected that all walls, furniture, fixtures, and equipment will have been included in the drawings and clearly identified. While it is not necessary to know the manufacturer of an individual piece of equipment in the restaurant, it is important to know what equipment is required, as well as the required dimensions and configuration.

Construction Documents
Also called "working drawings", this stage consists primarily of the mechanical, electrical, and plumbing (MEP) coordination required to make the building function. The "systems" within a building are very similar to those which exist in the body when you think about it – Structural (skeleton), Mechanical (breathing), Electrical (basis of cell communication and activity), plumbing, etc. This phase requires a significant amount of coordination between a large number of disciplines. It is an extremely important aspect of the design process, as a mistake at this stage can be very costly.

Specifications
Once the construction documents are completed, written specifications are developed to convey all information to the construction team. These specifications include details on the manufacturer, model number, and any required options for everything from the door hardware to the paint, and the flooring materials to the foodservice equipment. These specifications are then used by the construction team to gather pricing from general contractors and their sub-contractors. (See Figure 2.3, 2.4, 2.5, 2.6)

Figure 2.3, 2.4, 2.5, 2.6: Hand sketch and the realised open kitchen

2.2 Factors to Be Considered

Space Planning

"Getting into the nuances of space planning, for example, a 40 to 60-seater restaurant will need 800 to 1200 square feet (11.5 square metres) if it is a fast food operation or 1000 to 1500 square feet (139.4 square metres) if it is a fine dining," says Rao.

He also elaborates that, in the case of fine dining, however, the space specified above is devoid of area for the buffet counter for which another 150 square feet (14 square metres) of space would have to be added. Moreover, should the fine dining restaurant have an open kitchen, then 120 to 150 square feet (14 square metres) additional space would be required. Rao continues, "A bar which would just dispense would need about 80 to 100 sqare feet (7.4 to 9.3 square metres) space in addition to the space which has been mentioned above for the restaurant. Therefore in total, a fine dining restaurant of 40 seats with a buffet counter, display kitchen and a bar would amount to an area of approximately 1450 square feet (135 square metres)."

Layers of Activity

The visual impact of an open kitchen is significantly enhanced when there a variety of activity that occurs at different levels of depth perception. In other words, it looks really cool when there is a whole bunch of stuff going on simultaneously in different parts of the open kitchen. On way to achieve this is to incorporate pieces of equipment with constant activity. Rotisseries, open hearth ovens, charbroilers, and even six-burner ranges are good examples of equipment that have constant activity.

This concept can be taken a step further when the stations are strategically located. For instance, picture a display kitchen with a pick-up counter at the front, an expediter's station on the chef's side behind that counter, with an island cooking suite behind that (lots of activity there), and an open hearth oven with a constant flickering flame behind that. This layout has the potential for a variety of activity to occur simultaneously, one behind the other. This is the concept of "layers of activity". (See Figure 2.7, 2.8)

How's the View?

The objective of an open kitchen is to prepare food in front of the guest. It would make sense, then, that the open kitchen be located so that it can be easily viewed from the dining room. In certain scenarios it is appropriate for the kitchen to be visible from as much of the dining room as possible, while in other situations the kitchen may only be visible from a portion of the dining room. There is no right or wrong answer, rather such a decision depends on the overall concept. The location of the open kitchen, however, is an important issue that can affect the facility's design and should be addressed early in the design process.

2.7

2.8

Figure 2.7, 2.8: Layout plan of an open−kitchen restaurant

Flow

The importance of flow has to be addressed within a foodservice facility in depth. Flow is even more important for open kitchens, primarily because the interface between the service staff and kitchen staff occurs in full view of the dining area. Under normal circumstances, this interface can be chaotic at times.

In open kitchens, chaotic conditions simply are not an option. The service staff and kitchen staff need to meet, but never cross paths. The culinary staff should be able to access all support areas and produce their food without interruption from the servers. The servers, likewise, should be able to access all required areas without having to navigate the culinary staff. Because open kitchens are often divided, with some areas in full view and others concealed, achieving proper flow patterns can be more challenging than in traditional configurations. Proper consideration should be given to the final layout. (See Figure 2.9, 2.10)

A Happy Medium

Open kitchens, due to their intricate planning, configuration, and expense, do not typically provide a great deal of flexibility. Concealed, back-of-house kitchens are better suited for equipment configuration changes or substitutions. So, they can limit flexibility despite their higher costs. Fortunately, there is a happy medium when an open kitchen is desired but the cost and limitations are prohibitive.

Instead of having an entire kitchen in full view of the guest, it is possible to incorporate a remote display station within view from the dining area. The idea behind such a station is to offer the ambiance and interactivity unique to open kitchens, while limiting the expense and increasing the flexibility of the facility. In such a configuration, the main kitchen (i.e. hot and cold production, food pick-up areas, and service support stations) would remain in the back-of-house. Only a limited amount of production would be in view of the guest.

Dessert stations, for example, are well-suited for such a configuration. Picture a station with one or two culinary team members assembling desserts. Perhaps there is an open hearth oven for baked desserts to offer the constant activity desired. Guests will be able to see the chocolate sauce generously added to each plate and watch the chefs pull fresh baked desserts form the oven. Imagine the smell that would emulate from this station and drift throughout the dining room. Mission accomplished!

Figure 2.9, 2.10: Diners can enjoy the cooking process during having delicious food

Coordination

As we have seen, open kitchens can significantly enhance the dining experience when properly planned and coordinated. Open kitchens require a tremendous amount of coordination, as they feature unparalleled integration of form and function. If an open kitchen is to achieve its desired function, coordination is critical. Every detail must be analysed and conceptualised. When properly planned, open kitchens can be a feast for the eyes!

2.11

Aesthetic Component

The aesthetic component is important in open kitchens. When designed properly, even the support equipment and configuration takes into account what the guest will see, and how it looks. Storage areas will have be concealed or kept neat. Built-in equipment may be more desirable than free-standing equipment so that a finished look is achieved. Both the operation and construction budgets can be impacted by decisions made to accommodate the aesthetic objectives. (See Figure 2.11, 2.12)

Interior Finishing Materials

Due to extensive use of cooking oil and dried food, hazardous sources such as fuels and fuel gas and inflammable things such as furniture, decorations, curtains, tablecloths and carpets, when the open kitchen is connected with other parts of the restaurant, the fire is easy to spread quickly. In consideration of dinning places' specificities, it is recommended to select materials with high fire resistance as interior finishing materials to ensure safety. Besides incombustible materials used in ceiling, walls and floor, the rigorous control of the combustion performance of decorative materials, fabrics and furniture is especially important. The ceiling, walls and floor of dining area should use incombustible or nonflammable materials as possible. The selection of cables and wires, shells of electric equipment, fixed furniture such as tables, sofas and cabinets, carpets, curtains and decorative objects should conform to GB20286-2006 of China.

Figure 2.11,2.12: Delicate decoration of an open-kitchen restaurant

Chapter 3 :
Indoor Air Climate in Open Kitchen Restaurants

Today's food service operations are an experience for the senses. Dining in restaurants is more than a meal away from home; it is a carefully orchestrated show: the diners are the audience, the chefs are the stars, and the visible portion of the kitchen is the stage. The display/open kitchen has evolved into entertainment, a carefully choreographed hive of activity just a few feet from the table.

A comfortable indoor environment is a key factor in running a successful foodservice business and providing excellent service.In addition to the efficiency and functionality demands of traditional kitchens, display/ open kitchens pose a unique aesthetic and acoustic challenge as well as significant comfort demands for the benefit of guests.

Open kitchens are typically characterised by heavyload appliances located inside the dining area. When heavy cooking equipment is installed (grills, char broilers, satay grill, charcoal grill, Teppanyaki table, teriyaki grill etc...), a significant amount of oduour, smoke or noise can be generated in a very short time. What is most important is that the guests can enjoy the cooking show without being disturbed by cooking emissions or odours.（See Figure 3.1, 3.2）

3.1 Odour and Noise

3.1.1 Odour and Nuisance

Objectionable and offensive odours can cause significant adverse effects on people's lives and well being. Information on the odour nuisance from commercial kitchens is limited although the Chartered Institute of Environment Health (CIEH) has carried out surveys of Local Authorities to quantify the level of complaints made relating to odour nuisance in general. Table 3.1 lists the information gathered by the CIEH during the survey. The survey results:
· do not differentiate between types of industrial process;
· do not specifically identify commercial kitchens; and
· relate to all complaints received and not only "justified" complaints.

It is anticipated that odour problems associated with commercial kitchens will form only a small proportion of the complaints received but will form a significant proportion of the "premises subject to complaint".

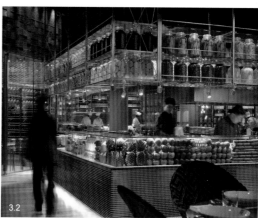

Figure3.1, 3.2: In the open kitchen, chefs illustrate step by step what they are cooking

Table 3.1 Results of CIEH survey of odour complaints attributed to industrial processes

Year	1998/1999	1999/2000
Complaints received	8,970	10,135
Complaints per million population	339	358
Premises subject to complaint	3,951	5,243
Notices served	80	60
Prosecutions	0	5
Convictions	0	5

Effects of odour
The main concern with odour is its ability to cause an effect that could be considered "objectionable or offensive". An objectionable or offensive effect can occur where an odorous compound is present in very low concentrations, usually far less than the concentration that could cause adverse effects on the physical health of humans or impacts on any other part of the environment.

Effects that have been reported by people include nausea, headaches, retching, difficulty breathing, frustration, annoyance, depression, stress, tearfulness, reduced appetite, being woken in the night and embarrassment in front of visitors. All of these contribute to a reduced quality of life for the individuals who are exposed.

Factors that influence magnitude of an odour problem
Factors that influence the control of odour from commercial kitchens include:
·Size of the cooking facility: This influences the intensity of the odour and volume of ventilation air to be handled.
·Type of food prepared: This affects the chemical constituents within the ventilation air.
·Type of cooking appliances used: This dictates the level of fat, water droplets and temperature within the ventilation air.

3.1.2 Noise and Nuisance
Noise is one of the main environmental problems in Europe, potentially affecting people's health and behaviour. Noise is generated by several types of source such as transport, indoor and outdoor equipment and industrial activity. In the case of commercial kitchens the noise generated by them can affect employees and the surrounding neighbourhood.

Information on the noise nuisance from commercial kitchens is limited. The CIEH have carried out surveys of Local Authorities to quantify the level of complaints made relating to noise nuisance in general. Table 3.2 lists the information for Commercial/Leisure activities for 2002-2003 in England and Wales. The survey results:

· do not differentiate between types of commercial/leisure activities;
· do not specifically identify commercial kitchens; and
· relate to all complaints received and not only "justified" complaints.

It is anticipated that noise problems associated with commercial kitchens will form only a small proportion of the complaints received and will also form a small proportion of the "sources complained of".

Table 3.2 Results of CIEH survey of noise complaints attributed to commercial/leisure activities in England and Wales (CIEH, 2003)

Category of noise nuisance	Commercial/leisure
Complaints received	40,602
Complaints per million population	1,014
Sources complained of	32,302
Sources confirmed as a nuisance	4,771
Nuisances remedied without notices being served	3,140
Notices served	1,310
Prosecutions	95
Convictions	48
Nuisances remedied by Local Authority in default	125

Types of noise in industrial kitchens

Factors that influence magnitude of noise in a commercial kitchen are:
·Size and format of the exhaust: The bulk flow leaving the exhaust diffuser generates broadband aero-acoustic noise. The sound level increases with increase in air speed and decreases with increase in area. The presence of grilles will generate tonal components. The sound levels are inversely proportional to the increase in area and increase with the eighth power of the flow speed.
·Heat release from kitchen: This influences the size of the exhaust system required and the flow rate of air to be handled by the system. Increase in flow rates can increase the pressure perturbations that can generate noise or can excite other parts of the system leading to noise.
·Type of cooking appliances used: this dictates the overall noise level as each individual appliance might contribute significantly to the total noise.
·Position of exhaust fan in the system: This may influence the noise radiated by the fan to the interior or exterior of the building and the transmission of sound energy into the exhaust duct system.
·Fitting and dimensions of the exhaust flow ducts: exhaust duct dimensions, fixings and insulation can all influence the amount of noise these structures will transmit and propagate. Selection of appropriate noise attenuating materials, avoidance of flow restrictions, and vibration isolators between the ducts and the fan are some of the aspects to be considered.
·Fan type and speed: Type of fan used (e.g. centrifugal fan with blades that are backward curved, forward curved or radial, or axial fan) will influence the level and nature of noise emitted. The fan characteristic needs to be chosen so that it is operating at its most efficient duty point as this tends to be the region of minimum noise. If fan speed is too high it will be operating away from that point which can lead to increases in level of up to 10 dB, as well as inefficient air management. It is often also desirable acoustically to use larger fans operating at low speeds rather than smaller fans operating at higher speeds. (See Table 3.3)

Table 3.3 Sources of noise from commercial kitchen ventilation systems

Source of Noise	How/Why Noise Arises
Extract hood	-High air velocities through extract hood
Extract/supply grille	-High air velocities through extract/supply grille
Extract/supply ductwork	-High air velocities through extract/supply ductwork -Resonance of fan noise through extract/supply ductwork
Extract/supply fan	-Fan motor noise -Fan impeller turning
Extract/supply discharge point	Convictions

3.2 Ventilation Systems (See Figure 3.3)

A number of Local Authorities have been contacted to review the types of problems encountered by Council Officers when dealing with odour and noise situations. Responses were received from metropolitan and rural Authorities. Authorities from England, Northern Ireland, Scotland and Wales have been consulted. The main areas of concern are summarised in Table 3.4

Figure 3. 3: Ventilation system in open-kitchen restaurant

Table 3.4 Summary of problems of commercial kitchen ventilation systems

Area	Effect
Where restaurant changes cooking type (e.g. from tea room to fish and chip shop)	Generally found that change introduces more extensive odour emissions over longer opening times. Existing planning permission may not include an odour control requirement. Need to rely on nuisance legislation to ensure mitigation measures are installed.
Application of carbon filtration	Mixed experience with carbon filters. Concerns about: · Poor maintenance; · Effect on back pressure leading to noise; · Effect on fan size leading to noise; and · Maintenance interval of 4 to 6 months considered appropriate always used in conjunction with stack for discharge.
UV/ozone systems	Limited experience with these systems. Concerns about: · Residual ozone always used in conjunction with high efficiency particulate removal and a stack.

Application of odour neutralising agents	Mixed experiences with this range of products. Concerns about: · Dosing levels leading to further odour problems; · On going maintenance. Can be used as a "polishing" technique in highly sensitive situations. Must be used in conjunction with stack.
Application of stack height	Mixed experience with stack heights. No consistency on appropriate height (roof eaves or ridge). Main concern occurred where: · Premises on rising ground where effective stack height is reduced; · Building housing premises is shorter than surrounding buildings; and · Premises is a listed building, is located in a conservation area or located in a courtyard.

The commercial kitchen is a unique space where many different HVAC applications take place within a single environment. Exhaust, supply, transfer, refrigeration, building pressurisation and air conditioning all must be considered in the design of most commercial kitchens.

It is obvious that the main activity in the commercial kitchen is the cooking process. This activity generates heat and effluent that must be captured and exhausted from the space in order to control odour and thermal comfort. The kitchen supply air, whether mechanical or transfer or a combination of both, should be of an amount that creates a small negative pressure in the kitchen space. This will avoid odours and

Figure 3.4: Heat gain and emission inside the kitchen

contaminated air escaping into surrounding areas. Therefore the correct exhaust air flow quantity is fundamental to ensure good system operation, thermal comfort and improved IAQ.

Similar considerations should be given to washing-up, food preparation and serving areas.

Initial Design Considerations
The modes of heat gain in a space may include solar radiation and heat transfer through the construction together with heat generated by occupants, lights and appliances and miscellaneous heat gains as air infiltration should also be considered.

Sensible heat (or dry heat) is directly added to the conditioned space by conduction, convection and radiation. Latent heat gain occurs when moisture is added to the space (e.g., from vapour emitted by the cooking process, equipment and occupants). Space heat gain by radiation is not immediate. Radiant energy must first be absorbed by the surfaces that enclose the space (walls, floor, and ceiling) and by the objects in the space (furniture, people, etc.). As soon as these surfaces and objects become warmer than the space air, some of the heat is transferred to the air in the space by convection. (See Figure 3.4).

To calculate a space cooling load, detailed building design information and weather data at selected design conditions are required. Generally, the following information is required:
· building characteristics
· configuration (e.g, building location)
· outdoor design conditions
· indoor design conditions
· operating schedules
· date and time of day

However, in commercial kitchens, cooking processes contribute the majority of heat gains in the space.

Heat Gain and Emissions Inside the Kitchen

Cooking can be described as a process that adds heat to food. As heat is applied to the food, effluent is released into the surrounding environment. This effluent release includes water vapour, organic material released from the food itself, and heat that was not absorbed by the food being cooked. Often, when pre-cooked food is reheated, a reduced amount of effluent is released, but water vapour is still emitted to the surrounding space.

The hot cooking surface (or fluid, such as oil) and products create thermal air currents (called a thermal plume) that are received or captured by the hood and then exhausted. If this thermal plume is not totally captured and contained by the hood, they become a heat load to the space.

There are numerous secondary sources of heat in the open kitchen (such as lighting, people, and hot meals) that contribute to the cooling load as presented in Table 3.5.

Table 3.5 Cooling load from various sources

Load	W
Lighting	21-54/m^2
People	130/person
Hot meal	15/meal
Cooking equipment	Varies
Refrigeration	Varies

Thermal Comfort, Productivity and Health

Thermal Comfort
One reason for the low popularity of kitchen work is the unsatisfactory thermal conditions.

Thermal comfort is a state where a person is satisfied with the thermal conditions.

The International Organisation for Standardisation (ISO) specifies such a concept as the predicted percentage of dissatisfied occupants (PPD) and the predicted mean vote (PMV) of occupants. PMV represents a scale from -3 to 3, from cold to hot, with 0 being neutral. PPD tells what percentage of occupants are likely to be dissatisfied with the thermal environment. These two concepts take into account four factors affecting thermal comfort: (See Figure 3.5)
· air temperature
· radiation
· air movement
· humidity

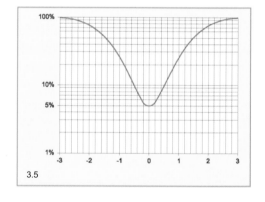

3.5

Figure 3.5: PPD as a function of PMV

The percentage of dissatisfied people remains under 10% in neutral conditions if the vertical temperature difference between the head and the feet is less than 3°C and there are no other non-symmetrical temperature factors in the space. A temperature difference of 6-8°C increases the dissatisfied percentage to 40-70%.

There are also important personal parameters influencing the thermal comfort (typical values in kitchen environment in parenthesis):
· clothing (0.5 - 0.8 clo)
· activity (1.6 - 2.0 met)

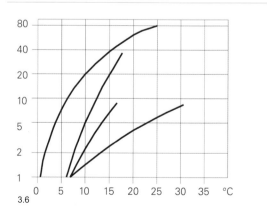

3.6

Figure 3.6: Assymmetric thermal radiation

Clo expresses the unit of the thermal insulation of clothing (1 clo = 0.155 m^2 K/W).

Met is a unit used to express the metabolic rate per unit Dubois area, defined as the metabolic rate of a sedentary person, 1 met = 50 kcal/(hr. m^2) = 58.2 W/m^2.

Assymmetric Thermal Radiation
In the kitchen, the asymmetry of radiation between the cooking appliances and the surrounding walls is considerable as the temperature difference of radiation is generally much higher than 20° C. (See Figure 3.6)

Ventilation Effectiveness and Air Distribution System

The Effect of Air Supply
Ventilation effectiveness can be described as the ability of ventilation system to achieve design conditions in the space (air temperature, humidity, concentration of impurities and air velocity) at minimum energy consumption. Air distribution methods used in the kitchen should provide adequate ventilation in the occupied zone, without disturbing the thermal plume.

In the commercial kitchen environment the supply airflow rate required to ventilate the space is a major factor contributing to the system energy consumption. Traditionally high velocity mixing or low velocity mixing systems have been used. Now there is a third alternative that clearly demonstrates improved thermal comfort over mixing systems, this is displacement ventilation.

The supply air (make-up air) can be delivered to the kitchen in two ways:
· high velocity or mixing ventilation
· low velocity or displacement

Low Velocity or Displacement Ventilation

Here, the cooler-than-surrounding supply air is distributed with a low velocity to the occupied zone. In this way, fresh air is supplied to where it is needed. Because of its low velocity, this supply air does not disturb the hood function. (See Figure 3.7)

High velocity or Mixing Ventilation
Everything that is released from the cooking process is mixed with the supply air. Obviously impurities and heat are mixed with surrounding air. Also the high velocity supply air disturbs the hood function. (See Figure 3.8) With a displacement system the intensity of turbulence of about 10 %, one accepts velocities between 0.25 and 0.40 m/s, with the air between 20 and 26°C respectively with 20% of people dissatisfied.

In the case of mixing ventilation, with an intensity of turbulence from 30 to 50 %, one finds 20 % of people dissatisfied in the following conditions: (See Table 3.6)

Productivity
Room air temperature affects a person's capacity to work. Comfortable thermal conditions decrease the number of accidents occurring in the work place. When the indoor temperature is too high (over 28 °C in commercial kitchens) the productivity and general comfort diminish rapidly.

The average restaurant spends about $2,000 yearly on salaries in the USA, wages and benefits per seat. If the air temperature in the restaurant is maintained at Picture 6. Productivity vs. Room Air Temperature 27°C in the kitchen the productivity of the restaurant employees is reduced to 80 %. That translates to losses of about $40,000 yearly on salaries and wages for an owner of a 100-seat restaurant. (See Figure 3.9)

Health
There are several studies dealing with cooking and health issues. The survey confirmed that cooking fumes contain hazardous components in both Western and Asian types of kitchens. In one study, the fumes

Figure 3. 7: Low velocity or displacement ventilation
With a displacement system the intensity of turbulence of about 10 %, one accepts velocities between 0.25 and 0.40 m/s, with the air between 20 and 26℃ respectively with 20% of people dissatisfied.

Figure 3.8: High velocity or mixing ventilation
In the case of mixing ventilation, with an intensity of turbulence from 30 to 50 %, one finds 20 % of people dissatisfied in the following conditions:

Table 3.6 Air temperature/air velocity

Air temperature. (℃)	20	26
Air velocity (m/s)	0.15	0.25

generated by frying pork and beef were found to be mutagenic. In Asian types of kitchens, a high concentration of carcinogens in cooking oil fumes has been discovered. All this indicates that kitchen workers may be exposed to a relatively high concentration of airborne impurities and that cooks are potentially exposed to relatively high levels of mutagens and carcinogens.

Chinese women are recognised to have a high incidence of lung cancer despite a low smoking rate e.g. only 3% of women smoke in Singapore. The studies carried out show that inhalation of carcinogens generated during frying of meat may increase the risk of lung cancer.

The risk was further increased among women stirfrying meat daily whose kitchens were filled with oily fumes during cooking. Also, the statistical link between chronic coughs, phlegm and breathlessness on exertion and cooking were found.

In addition to that, Cinni Little states, that three quarters of the population of mainland China alone use diesel as fuel type instead of town gas or LPG, causing extensive bronchial and respiratory problems among kitchen workers, which is possibly exacerbated by an air stream introduced into the burner mix.

Reduction of Health Impact
The range of thermal comfort neutrality acceptable without any impact on health has been proposed as running between 17°C as the lowest and 31°C as the highest acceptable temperature (Weihe 1987, quoted in WHO 1990). Symptoms of discomfort and health risks outside this range are indicated in Table 3.7.

Figure 3. 9: Productivity vs. Room Air Temperature

Table 3.7 Health effects of thermal microclimates lying outside the neutral comfort zone

	<17°C	>31°C	
Sudden heart death	Hypertension	Hypotension	Sudden heart death
Stroke	Hypertension	Hyperthermia	Heart failure
	Respiratory infections	Tachycardia	Heat stroke
	Asthma	Health insufficiency	
	Overheating	Inappetence	
	Tachycardia	Hypohydrosis	
	Reduced dexterity	Hydromeiosis	
	Indolecense	Indolence	
	Restlessness	Fatigue	
	Mental slowing	Lethargy	
	Depression	Increased irritability	

Ventilation Rate

The airflow and air distribution methods used in the kitchen should provide adequate ventilation in the occupied zone, without disturbing the thermal plume as it rises into the hood system. The German VDI-2052 standard states that a:

Ventilation rate over 40 vol./h result on the basis of the heat load, may lead to draughts.

The location of supply and exhaust units are also important for providing good ventilation. Ventilating systems should be designed and installed so that the ventilation air is supplied equally throughout the occupied zone. Some common faults are to locate the supply and exhaust units too close to each other, causing "short-circuiting" of the air directly from the supply opening to the exhaust openings. Also, placing the high velocity supply diffusers too close to the hood system reduces the ability of the hood system to provide sufficient capture and containment (C&C) of the thermal plume.

Recent studies show that the type of air distribution system utilised affects the amount of exhaust needed to capture and contain the effluent generated in the cooking process.

Integrated Approach

Energy savings can be realised with various exhaust hood applications and their associated make-up air distribution methods. However with analysis the potential for increased energy savings can be realised when both extract and supply for the kitchen are adopted as an integrated system.

The combination of high efficiency hoods and displacement ventilation reduces the required cooling capacity, while maintaining temperatures in the occupied space. The natural buoyancy characteristics of the displacement air helps the C&C of the contaminated convective plume by 'lifting' it into the hood. (See Figure 3.10)

Third-party research has demonstrated that this integrated approach for the kitchen has the potential to provide the most efficient and lowest energy consumption of any kitchen system available today. (See Figure 3.10)

Figure 3.10: Displacement ventilation

3.3 Kitchen Hoods

The purpose of kitchen hoods is to remove the heat, smoke, effluent, and other contaminants. The thermal plume from appliances absorbs the contaminants that are released during the cooking process. Room air replaces the void created by the plume. If convective heat is not removed directly above the cooking equipment, impurities will spread throughout the kitchen, leaving discoloured ceiling tiles and greasy countertops and floors. Therefore, contaminants from stationary local sources within the space should be controlled by collection and removal as close to the source as is practical.

Appliances contribute most of the heat in commercial kitchens. When appliances are installed under an effective hood, only the radiant heat contributes to the HVAC load in the space. Conversely, if the hood is not providing sufficient capture and containment, convective and latent heat are "spilling" into the kitchen thereby increasing both humidity and temperature.

Capture efficiency is the ability of the kitchen hood to provide sufficient capture and containment at a minimum exhaust flow rate.

3.3.1 Selecting & Sizing Exhaust Hoods
Fundamentals of Kitchen Exhaust
An exhaust fan in the ceiling could remove much of the heat produced by cooking equipment. But mix in smoke, volatile organic compounds, grease particles and vapor from cooking, and a means to capture and contain the effluent becomes necessary to avoid health and fire hazards. While an exhaust hood serves that purpose, the key question becomes: what is the appropriate exhaust rate? The answer always depends on several factors: the menu of food products and the type (and use) of the cooking equipment under the hood, the style and geometry of the hood itself, and how the makeup air (conditioned or otherwise) is introduced into the kitchen.

The Cooking Factor

Cooking appliances are categorized as light-, medium-, heavy-, and extra heavy-duty, depending on the strength of the thermal plume and the quantity of grease, smoke, heat, water vapor, and combustion products produced. The strength of the thermal plume is a major factor in determining the exhaust rate. By their nature, these thermal plumes rise by natural convection, but they are turbulent and different cooking processes have different "surge" characteristics. For example, the plume from hamburger cooking is strongest when flipping the burgers. Ovens and pressure fryers may have very little plume until they are opened to remove food product. Open flame, non-thermostatically controlled appliances, such as underfired broilers and open top ranges, exhibit strong steady plumes. Thermostatically controlled appliances, such as griddles and fryers have weaker plumes that fluctuate in sequence with thermostat cycling (particularly gas-fired equipment). As the plume rises, it should be captured by the hood and removed by the suction of the exhaust fan. Air in the proximity of the appliances and hood moves in to replace it. This replacement air, which must ultimately originate as outside air, is referred to as makeup air.

Building codes distinguish between cooking processes that create smoke and grease (e.g., frying, griddling, or charbroiling) and those that produce only heat and moisture (e.g., dishwashing and some baking and steaming operations). Cooking that produces smoke and grease requires liquid-tight construction with a built-in fire suppression system (Type I hood), while operations that produce only heat and moisture do not require liquid-tight construction or a fire sup-pression system (Type II hood).

Menu items may produce more or less smoke and grease depending on their fat content and how they are cooked. Higher fat content foods tend to re-lease more smoke and grease regardless of the type of cooking process. Testing under an ASHRAE sponsored research project at the University of Minnesota confirmed that hamburger cooked on a charbroiler releases finer smoke parti-cles and more grease vapour and particles than hamburger cooked on a griddle. The percentage fat content of hamburger also contributes to differences in the amount of grease and smoke released in cooking. Chicken breast, which has less fat compared to hamburger, releases less particulate and less grease during cooking on a charbroiler or on a griddle compared to hamburger.

The Hood Factor

The design exhaust rate also depends on the hood style and construction features. Wall-mounted canopy hoods, island (single or double) canopy hoods, and proximity (backshelf, pass-over, or eyebrow) hoods all have different capture areas and are mounted at different heights and horizontal positions relative to the cooking equipment. Generally, for the identical (thermal plume) challenge, a single-island canopy hood requires more exhaust than a wall-mounted canopy hood, and a wall-mounted canopy hood requires more exhaust than a proximity (backshelf) hood. The performance of a double-island canopy tends to emulate the performance of two back-to-back wall-canopy hoods, although the lack of a physical barrier between the two hood sections makes the configuration more susceptible to cross drafts.

Building and/or health codes typically provide basic construction and materials requirements for exhaust hoods, as well as prescriptive exhaust rates based on appliance duty and length of the hood (cfm per linear ft.) or open face area of the hood (cfm per ft^2). Codes usually recognize exceptions for hoods that have been tested against a recognized standard, such as Underwriters Laboratories (UL) Standard 710. Part of the UL standard is a "cooking smoke and flair up" test. This test is essentially a cooking effluent capture and containment (C&C) test where "no evidence of smoke or flame escaping outside the exhaust hood" must be observed. Hoods bearing a recognized laboratory mark are called listed hoods, while those constructed to the prescriptive requirements of the building code are called unlisted hoods. Generally, an off-the-shelf listed hood can be operated at a lower exhaust rate than an unlisted hood of comparable style and size over the same cook line. Lower exhaust rates may be proven by labora-tory testing with specific hood(s) and appliance lineup using the test protocol described in ASTM Standard

F-1704, Test Method for Performance of Commercial Kitchen Ventilation Systems. This process is sometimes referred to as "custom-engineering" a hood.

Laboratory testing of different combinations of appliances has demonstrated that minimum capture and containment rates vary significantly due to appliance type and position under the hood. For example a heavy-duty appliance at the end of a hood is more prone to spillage than the same appliance located in the middle of the hood. (See Figure 3.11)

3.11

Figure 3.11: Styles of exhaust hoods

Side Panels and Overhang

Side (or end) panels permit a reduced ex-haust rate in most cases, as all of the replacement air is drawn across the front of the equipment, which improves containment of the effluent plume generated by the hot equipment. They are a relatively inexpensive way to improve C&C and reduce the total exhaust rate. Another benefit of end panels is to mitigate the negative effect that cross drafts can have on hood performance. It is important to know that partial side panels can provide almost the same benefit as full panels. Although tending to defy its definition as an "island" canopy, end panels can improve the performance of a double-island or single-island canopy hood.

An increase in overhang should improve the ability of a canopy hood to capture because of the increased distance between the plume and hood edges. This may be accomplished by pushing the appliances as far back under a canopy hood as practical and/or by increasing the side length. Although this improves C&C performance, for unlisted hoods under a local jurisdiction referencing the Uniform Mechanical Code (UMC), this would require increase in the code-required exhaust rate. Larger overhangs are recommended for appliances that create plume surges, such as convection and combination ovens, steamers and pressure fryers. This was the driving argument for converting the code-specified exhaust rates from a "cfm/ft^2" to a "cfm/linear ft". basis in the cur-rent edition of the International Mechanical Code (IMC). (See Figure 3.12)

Hood Geometry

The ability of a hood to capture and contain cooking effluent can often be enhanced by adding passive features (e.g., angles, flanges, or geometric flow deflectors) or active features (e.g., low-flow, high-velocity jets) along the edges of the hood or within the hood reservoir. Such design features can improve hood performance dramatically over a basic box-style hood with the same nominal dimensions.

3.12

Figure 3.12: Illustration of partial and full side panels

Cross Drafts

Cross drafts can have a detrimental affect on all hood/appliance combinations. Cross drafts affect island canopy hoods more than wall mounted canopy hoods because they have more open area allowing drafts to push or pull effluent from the hood. For example, a pedestal fan used by staff for additional cooling can severely degrade hood performance, may make capture impossible and may spill the plume into the kitchen. Location of delivery doors, service doors, pass-through openings and drive-through windows may be sources of cross drafts due to external and internal air pressure differences. Cross drafts can also be developed when the makeup air system is not working correctly, causing air to be pulled from open drive-through windows or doors.

The Makeup Factor

The layout of the heating, ventilating, and air-conditioning (HVAC) and makeup air (MUA) supply air outlets or diffusers can affect hood performance. These can be sources that disrupt thermal plumes and hinder C&C. Safety factors are typically applied to the design exhaust rate to compensate for the effect that undesired air movement within the kitchen has on hood performance.

Air that is removed from the kitchen through an exhaust hood must be replaced with an equal volume of outside replacement (makeup) air through one or more of the following pathways:
1. Transfer air (e.g., from the dining room)
2. Displacement diffusers (floor or wall mounted)
3. Ceiling diffusers with louvers (2-way, 3-way, 4-way)
4. Slot diffusers (ceiling)
5. Ceiling diffusers with perforated face
6. Integrated hood plenum including:
· Short circuit (internal supply)
· Air curtain supply
· Front face supply
· Perforated perimeter supply
· Backwall supply (rear discharge)

· Combinations of the above

The Design Process

Successfully applying the fundamentals of commercial kitchen ventilation (CKV) during the design process requires a good understanding of the local building code requirements, the menu and appliance preferences, and the project's budget. Information about the kitchen equipment and ventilation requirements may evolve over the course of the design phase. Data needed by other members of the design team may require early estimates of certain parameters (e.g., the amount of exhaust and makeup air, motor horsepower, water supply and wastewater flow rates). As more decisions are made, new information may allow (or require) refinements to the design that affect exhaust and makeup air requirements.

The fundamental steps in the design of a CKV system are:
1. Establish location and "duty" classifications of appliances including menu effects. Determine (or coordinate with food service consultant) preferred appliance layout for optimum exhaust ventilation.
2. Select hood type, style, and features.
3. Size exhaust airflow rate.
4. Select makeup air strategy, size airflow and layout diffusers.

A good understanding of how building code requirements apply to kitchen design is essential. Local or state building codes are usually based on one of the "model" building codes promulgated by national code organisations. Our discussion of the building codes will be limited to require-ments that affect design exhaust and makeup air rates, which are usually found in the mechanical code portion of the overall building code.

Historically, codes and test standards used "temperature" ratings for classifying cooking equipment. Although these temperature ratings roughly correlated with the ventilation requirement of the appliances, there were many gray areas. During development of ASHRAE Standard 154, Ventilation for Commercial Cooking Appliances, it was recognised that plume strength, which takes into account plume volume and surge characteristics, as well as plume tempera-ture, would be a better measure for rating appliances for application in building codes. "Duty" ratings were created for the majority of commercial cooking appliances under Standard 154, and these were recently adopted by the International Mechanical Code (IMC). The Kitchen Ventilation chapter of the ASHRAE Applications Handbook (2003 edition) applied the same concept to establish ranges of exhaust rates for listed hoods. The appended Design Exam-ples in this Guide reference duty classifications for appliances. The duty classifications listed in the sidebar are from ASHRAE Standard 154-2003, Ventilation for Commercial Cooking Operations.

The IMC dictates exhaust rates based on hood type and appliance duty. Table 3.8 states these exhaust rates in "cfm per linear foot of hood" ("linear foot" in this case applies to the distance from edge to edge along the front face of the hood). The Code requires that the exhaust rate for the highest duty-rated appliance be applied to the entire hood. The Uniform Mechanical Code (UMC), used in many California jurisdictions, requires calculating exhaust rates based on square-footage of capture area (capture area is the open area defined by the lower edges of the hood). The UMC uses temperature classifications for appliances, as described above. Both the IMC and the UMC require a minimum 6-inch hood overhang (front and sides) for canopy style hoods.

Table 3.8 Unlisted Hood Exhaust Flow Rates

Minimum Exhaust Flow Rate for Unlisted Hoods (cfm per linear foot of hood)				
Type of Hood	Light Duty Equipment	Medium Duty Equipment	Heavy Duty Equipment	Extra-Heavy Duty Equipment
Wall-mounted Canopy	200	300	400	550
Single Island Canopy	400	500	600	700
Double Island Canopy	250	300	400	550
Eye Brow	250	250	not allowed	not allowed
Backshelf	250	300	400	not allowed
Passover	250	300	400	not allowed

The prescriptive mechanical code exhaust rate requirements must be conservative because the AHJ (authority having jurisdiction) has no control over the design of an exhaust hood or the positioning and diversity of appliances placed beneath that hood. However, in cases where the CKV system design and appliance configuration has been optimised, the code-specified exhaust rate may be significantly greater than what is required for effective capture and containment of the cooking plume. The code-based safety factor (which may be necessary for unlisted systems) can place an energy cost burden on the CKV system through its demand for more heated and cooled makeup air.

When the energy crisis of the 1970's occurred, kitchen ventilation systems became an obvious target. Industry responded with two methods of reducing the amount of replacement air that had to be cooled or heated: (1) short-circuit hoods, and (2) listed hoods.

One strategy, called "internal compensation," was to introduce the makeup air directly into the hood reservoir. This is more commonly known as "short-circuit" makeup air. Although short-circuit hoods have been installed and operated with as much as 80% of replacement air being introduced internally, field and laboratory investigations have shown that these hoods fail to capture and contain effluent adequately.

The second industry strategy was to test hoods under laboratory conditions according to a test protocol specified by Underwriters Laboratories, Standard 710, Exhaust Hoods for Commercial Cooking Equipment. This UL Standard covers materials and construction of exhaust hoods as well as C&C performance. The C&C performance is based on testing a single appliance under a representative hood at one or more of three cooking temperature operating set points (400°F, 600°F, or 700°F). The UL listing reports the minimum C&C rate determined under this laboratory test.

Another American national standard, ASTM Standard F-1704-1999, Test Method for Performance of Commercial Kitchen Ventilation Systems, covers exhaust hood capture and containment performance as well as heat gain from hooded appliances. The current version of ASTM F-1704 also does not address dynamic conditions, but there are amendments under consideration to add a dynamic test that would quantify a safety factor. The capture and containment tests in UL 710 and ASTM F-1704 are similar.

While the exhaust rates shown in Table 3.8 are minimum mandatory rates for unlisted hoods, the rates in Table 3.9 reflect the typical range in design exhaust rates for listed hoods. The values in this table may be useful for estimating the "cfm" advantage offered by listed hoods over unlisted hoods for a given project. But in the final stage of design, exhaust rates may be adjusted to account for:

1. Diversity of operations (how many of the appliances will be on at the same time).
2. Position under the hood (appliances with strong thermal plumes, located at the end of a hood, tend to spill effluent more easily than the same appliance located in the middle of the hood).
3. Hood overhang (in combination with appliance push-back). Positioning a wall-mounted canopy hood over an appliance line with an 18-inch overhang can dramatically reduce the required ventilation rate when compared to the minimum overhang requirement of 6 inches. Some manufacturers "list" their hoods for a minimum 12-inch overhang, providing an immediate advantage over unlisted hoods.
4. Appliance operating temperature (e.g. a griddle used exclusively by a multi-unit restaurant at 325°F vs. 400°F surface temperature) or other specifics of appliance design (e.g. 18-inch vs. 24-inch deep griddle surface).
5. Differences in effluent from menu selections, such as cooking hamburger on a griddle versus on a charboiler, or using a charboiler to cook chicken versus hamburger.
6. Operating experience of a multi-unit restaurant can be factored into the equation. For example, the CKV system design exhaust rate (for the next new restaurant) may be increased or decreased based on real-world assessments of the CKV system in recently constructed facilities.

Table 3.9 Typical Exhaust Rates for Listed Hoods

Minimum Exhaust Flow Rate for Listed Hoods (cfm per linear foot of hood)				
Type of Hood	Light Duty Equipment	Medium Duty Equipment	Heavy Duty Equipment	Extra-Heavy Duty Equipment
Wall-mounted Canopy	150-200	200-300	200-400	350+
Single Island Canopy	250-300	300-400	300-600	550+
Double Island Canopy	150-200	200-300	250-400	500+
Eye Brow	150-250	150-250	not recommended	not recommended
Back-shelf/Passover	100-200	200-300	300-400	not recommended

3.4 Ventilated Ceiling

General

The ventilated ceiling is an alternative kitchen exhaust system. The ceiling should be used for aesthetic reasons when open space is required, multiple kitchen equipment of different types is installed and the kitchen floor space is large.

The ventilated ceilings are used in Europe especially in institutional kitchens like schools and hospitals.

Ceilings are categorised as "Open" and "Closed" ceiling system.

3.4.1 Open Ceiling
Principle
Open ceiling is the design with suspended ceiling that consists of a supply and exhaust area.

Supply and exhaust air ductworks are connected to the voids above the suspended ceiling. Open ceiling is usually assembled from exhaust and supply cassettes.

The space between the ceiling and the void is used as a plenum. The contaminated air goes via the slot where grease and particles are separated. (See Figure 3.13)

Figure 3.13: Open ceiling

Specific Advantages
· Good aesthetics.
· Possibility to change kitchen layout.

Disadvantages
· Not recommended for heavy load (gas griddle, broiler).

Figure 3.14: Closed ceiling

3.14

· Efficient when only steam is produced.
· Not recommended from a hygienic point of view (free space above the ceiling used as plenum – risk of contamination).
· Expensive in maintenance.
· Condensation risk.

3.4.2 Closed Ceiling (See Figure 3.14)
Halton ventilated ceiling is based on Capture Jet™ installed flush to the ceiling surface, which helps to guide the heat and impurities towards the extract sections. Supply air is delivered into the kitchen through a low velocity unit.

Air distribution significantly affects thermal comfort and the indoor air quality in the kitchen. There are also combinations of hoods and ventilated ceilings. Heavy frying operations with intensive grease emission are considered to be a problem for ventilated ceilings, so hoods are recommended instead.

Principle
Supply and exhaust units are connected straight to the ductwork. This system consists of having rows of filter and supply units; the rest is covered with infill panel.

There are various closed ceilings. For example, Halton utilise the most efficient ceiling, which includes an exhaust equipped with a high efficiency KSA filter, supply air unit and a Capture JetTM system installed flush to the ceiling panels.

Specific Advantages
· Draught free air distribution into the working zone. from low velocity ceiling mounted panels.
· High efficiency grease filtration using Halton KSA "Multi-cyclone" filters.
· Protection of the building structure from grease, humidity and impurities.
· Modular construction simplifies design, installation and maintenance.
· Integrated Capture Jets within supply air sections.

Chapter 4:
Case Studies

An Open Kitchen Is to Entertain Diners

–Words from designer of Studio Arthur Casas in restaurant design

Sao Paulo is a City that reveals itself behind the walls which makes some places amazing and special. I have noticed a pleasant change in the restaurants of the hotels, especially those completed in the last five years. These places have their own personalities, many times even completely different from the hotels where they are in, with independent entrances when it's possible, and personally I don't see many substantial differences between freestanding restaurants and hotels restaurants.

In my opinion it's absolutely unnecessary to decor restaurants and shops with arts and regarding the colours and materials. I prefer the warm ones (red, orange) and natural materials like stone, brick, wood. They refer to the "affective memory".

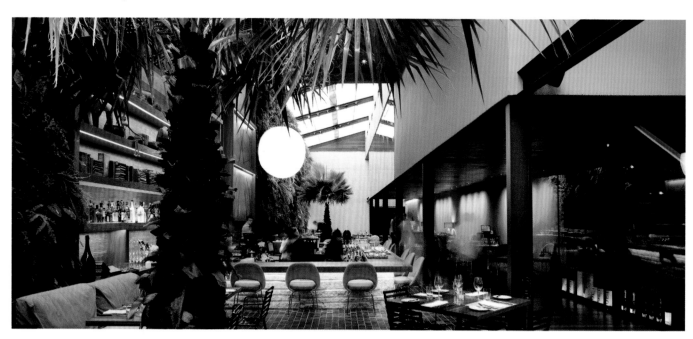

The discrete façade of the newest restaurant KAA gives no hint of what may prove to be internally. Inside, the narrow space of 798 m^2 gets a new depth through the Green vertical wall with plants from the Atlantic forest. The water mirror on the bottom of the tropical green wall refers to "Igarapés", that were so common before as well as nowadays in that region.

The huge stand at the bar that divides the big environment of the restaurant in 2 separate areas is to support indigenous original pieces which mimic with the bottles, cups and books. The roof made with canvas opens automatically. The furniture is contemporary and the philosophy of this place is transporting the urban "Paulista" to a green environment. It's an escape from the chaos.

People go to restaurants not only for food but also for entertainment, to surprise themselves, out of their normal working environment and their residences. More and more people's concerns regard to the origin of the food and how it is made. The light must be the right one; the place can't be or looks too large; the neighbour can't hear your conversation; the music must be appropriate; the sound impeccable; a comfortable chair and the table on the correct height. I prefer to see the chef working and if possible choose my wine in the cellar.

I'm not fanatic for technology and I don't believe that people seek for technology when they are in bars and restaurants. If there are technologies it should be in a natural and harmonious way. I really think, especially when we dealing with a restaurant, what people seek is for a kind of "affective memory" of grandmother's house, of a garden, of a mom's kitchen.

(All images are of KAA in São Paulo designed by Studio Arthur Casas and photographed by Leonardo Finotti)

The Drama of an Open Kitchen

Wolfgang Puck practically invented the phenomenon of cooking in front of diners in 1982, Michael Ruhlman wrote in his book, "Reach of a Chef" – it is a claim that discounts Japanese sushi chefs but whatever. What's indisputable is that foodies like to watch food being made.

Feedback from the Super diners, which San Diego open-kitchen restaurant does good theater and good plates?

The chefs they are culinary artists: cultured, creative and graceful.
> — Susan Russo, cookbook author, blogger (foodblogga.blogspot.com)

This year, it has been Searsucker, where Brian Malarkey's "Top Chef" personality comes through. Dine at the kitchen bar and observe the conductor of the food opera. (Editor's note: He's conducting up at his new restaurant Burlap, too.)
> — Randee Stratton, real estate broker, avid diner

I hate to brag, but I opened one of the first open-kitchen restaurants in town. It is still here and it still serves food (and sushi, too): Sally's Seafood on the Water at the Manchester Grand Hyatt downtown. Chef Sarah Linkenheil serves great food right on the marina, and, as a matter of fact, you can even eat in the kitchen. (But can you stand the heat?) My other favorite is Delicias (6106 Paseo Delicias, Rancho Santa Fe. (858) 756-8000; deliciasrestaurant.com), also one of the oldest restaurant in town with an open kitchen. And guess who was involved with Delicias 20 years ago? Wolfgang Puck! (Editors note: Puck helped open the original Delicias.)

— Fabrice Poigin, private chef, restaurant consultant

Easy Super Cocina (3627 University Ave., Normal Heights. (619) 584-6244; supercocinasd.com). Although it's a cafeteria setup, anyone in line can see the prep and kitchen area clearly. If you're not familiar with a particular guisado (a stew) or just want to taste, simply ask for a sample. That's all the theatre I need.

— Matthew Rowley, food historian, blogger (whiskeyforge.com; Twitter @mbrowley)

I don't know about good theatre, but the open kitchen at Jsix is pretty cool. They recently remodeled their dining room. We had the Chef's Mercy menu there a few weeks ago. Chef Christian Graves cooks up some good meat.

— Robin Taylor, organic farmer at Suzie's Farm and Sun Grown Organic Distributors

When I am paying attention, Dolce Pane e Vino (16081 San Dieguito Road, Rancho Santa Fe. (858) 832-1518; dolcepaneevino.com) seems to keep me looking. I enjoy watching the harmony with which all the cooks in the tiny kitchen are able to produce such good food and not trip all over each other.

— Dave Morgan, CPA, avid diner

Although not classically an open kitchen, there is action behind the counter in the staging area at Kitchen 1540 at L'Auberge Del Mar. Watch as Chef Paul McCabe plates and serves some of the best local ingredients and most original food in San Diego.

> — Charles Kaufman, baker, owner of Bread & Cie Café

Having never worked in a restaurant, I am fascinated with all kitchen operations, because it is so foreign to me. The most entertaining kitchen I have seen recently is at Searsucker on a busy night. There is nothing like watching Brian Malarkey yell out orders. The other night I found myself captivated, ignoring my dinner guests, watching the kitchen work like a well-oiled machine. I never did figure out who was listening to Brian's orders, but everything seemed to be working flawlessly.

> — David Salisbury, a law firm's director of business development, avid diner

My first Searsucker dining experience started off with us showing up without reservations. The only seating available was at the kitchen counter in full view of the sous chefs and pastry chef working their magic in the open kitchen. They were very personable and to see them prep their amazing dishes was quite the treat.

> — Joanne Arellano, human resources professional, avid Yelper, avid diner

Kitchen 1540: I like the setup, it fits the room perfectly.

> — William Bradley, executive chef at Addison

I have seen the likes of Emeril Lagasse and Bobby Flay in action, which was a treat. But the best interloping I have been party to involves aproned guys whose names I do not know, whom I have glimpsed when they were not looking. That said, it is fun to watch Brian Malarkey holler to his kitchen commandos at Searsucker. I like getting a peek of the linemen at L'Auberge Del Mar's KITCHEN 1540. And I, like most local foodies, cannot wait to see Matt Gordon's crew at work from the special table that'll be built at Encinitas' upcoming Solace and the Moonlight Lounge.

— Brandon Hernández, food writer (Twitter @offdutyfoodie)

Our farmer's markets offer all kinds of tent-kitchen-theare excitement! The plethora of sensory stimuli that comes with this kind of picnic-nosh-meal makes the experience, I think. The smells of a grill burning and all the different foods cooking; the sounds of children laughing and running around; the feeling of being outside with the sun kissing skin, all the visual delights, and of course, the delicious. Good theatre, good plates! Searsucker, the pizza station at Cucina Urbana and Bread and Cie, too!

— Tina Luu, pastry chef, food lecturer at the Art Institute of California San Diego

When I was little, I was fascinated by flaming tableside preparations of beef and duck at Chinese restaurants. How I did not become a pyromaniac, I will never know! But these days, I keep it simple: barbacoa burrito at Chipotle. It is so exciting how they spread that medium-heat salsa and sprinkle that queso.

— Gerald "Dex" Poindexter, publicist, avid diner

Kitchen 1540: Cannot wait to see where Chef Paul McCabe takes us on his next culinary ride.

— Andrew Spurgin, chef/partner Campine – A Culinary + Cocktail Conspiracy

I gravitate to exhibition kitchens and chef's counters in every city I visit. On our way to Tuscaloosa for a reunion? You can bet we'll be at Hot & Hot Fish Club in Birmingham to watch Chris Hastings at work. But we don't have a favorite here, at least since that once upon a time when Nathan Coulon starred at Quarter Kitchen. Don't tell Brian, but I still haven't eaten at Searsucker, though I hear good things. Does Kono's Café count? Because watching that crew move the number of eggs and trays of bacon that they do through that tiny kitchen is poetry in motion.

— Catt White, farmers' market manager (Twitter @LIMercato)

Muvenpick

Completion date: 2009
Location: Zurich, Switzerland
Designer: Stephen Williams Associates
Photos: Mövenpick Hotel Zurich–Airport
Area: 300m²

September 2009 marked the opening of the Mövenpick Restaurant in the Mövenpick Hotel Zürich Airport. Earlier, in February 2009 architects at Stephen Williams Associates, Hamburg, were chosen to take on the project. After five months of planning and advertising and a 20-day construction period, SWA had the restaurant ready for occupancy and could open the doors for business. These establishments were produced, supplied and installed by the international restaurant-fitter Reinhold Keller, Kleinheubach, whose enterprise has already established more than 3,000 restaurants world-wide in just the past few years.

Mövenpick's President and CEO, Jean Gabriel Peres, congratulates with the words: "This is another showcase which sets a trend for future concepts: warm, smart-casual, interactive but quality oriented, I really like it but more importantly the guest feedback is very positive."

The open kitchen is located at the entrance and diners can appreciate it once stepping into the restaurant.

1. Entrance
2. High table
3. Lounge
4. Dim sum
5. Pavilion
6. Separee
7. Flexibel
8. Separee

Floor Plan

The approximate 300m² large surface is separated into six parts with different seat typologies: from low lounge furniture to flexible two- and four-seater tables through to six-seater seating areas and high-tables with bar stools. Each seating combination is suitable for any situation: whether for breakfast, lunch, coffee or dinner, for groups, pairs or those visiting alone – every seat conveys the feeling of being the best. Standing centrally is an L-shaped counter created out of copper. It is here that the meals are prepared in copper pots and pans directly in front of the eyes of the guests. The food is presented on a counter with a copper-tiled base situated below a lintel which is plastered with a coppery metal coating.

Warm walnut, red- and beige-coloured upholstery together with glass panels inlaid with grass help to enhance the freshness and quality of the gastronomy on offer at Mövenpick. Historical black and white photographs of the Zurich-born aerialview photographer Walter Mittelholzer remind the guest of the wonders of aviation and travel. It is not only the hotel guests, but also the regular Mövenpick customers who are impressed by the new interior design.

Restaurant Kaskada

Completion date: 2010
Location: Liberec, Czech Republic
Designer: maura I Mark é ta Veselá, Alena Nováčková
Area: 313m²

The new restaurant was designed for the empty un-used space, next to the cinema multi-complex, in the Nisa shopping centre in Liberec. The investor convinced the designers about the concept of cooking in front of the guests. The restaurant is visually separated from the shopping area by a strip of lowered ceiling. The maximum height of the restaurant space is preserved and is enhanced by decorated bespoke panelling.

1. Entrance
2. Open kitchen
3. Dining area
4. Bathroom

Floor Plan

The interior of the restaurant is clearly visible from the entrance. The area is divided into three parts: the restaurant, the bar and technical facilities concealed behind a wall on the left side of the restaurant. The cooking area is connected with the restaurant space by a narrow horizontal window, making the whole operation of the kitchen clearly visible and allowing patrons to take a peek at the chefs at work. Diagonal to the kitchen is the dishwashing area and a long corridor with preparation areas and storage. A single stairway leads to the floor with facilities for employees.

The main motif of the wooden panelling is based on the name of the restaurant. The aesthetic panelling of the central column of the restaurant also reflects the motif. Here, the wooden panels on two sides of the column conceal storage. Visitors can instantly see the elegant silhouette of the letter "K", enhanced by illuminated glass, affixed to the column. In addition to wooden panelling, another important material incorporated is roughly stacked sabre slate forming low partitioning walls between the tables, the bar wall and the rear wall of the restaurant. The remaining surfaces of the lowered ceiling are painted in an anthracite tone and the cream coloured walls are livened up with graphic printing again based on the letter "K".

Ellas Melathron Aromata

Completion Date: 2011
Location: Athens, Greece
Designer: Minas Kosmidis
Photos: Ioanna Roufopoulou
Area: Inside 214m², Balcony 97m², Open Space 190m²

Ellas Melathron Aromata is located at the shopping centre of Smart Park at Spata of Attica, in Greece. The concept of this alternative coffee-candy-fast food shop was the creation of a space with intense scent, flavours and atmosphere of urban Greece in the early 50's and 60's.

The store is developed on three floors. In the ground floor there are the principal services for the public, while the living room expands on the first floor. At the basement there are the ancillary areas, the main kitchen and the toilets, while the store expands with tables and chairs on a covered outdoor patio, which is bordered by vertical wooden beams that form the perimeter and the other sedentary. The pergola has panels fitted with digital prints and rosettes with hanging lights to illuminate the exterior.

The open kitchen is located on the ground floor, which can be seen from outside through the glass façade as well. The diners can enjoy the skillful performance of the chef while having their delicious food.

Dining areas on the ground floor are separated and furnished in different styles. The intense Greek character is underlined by the traditional minimarket-like booth. Other elements adding to the scenic appearance of the environment are the handmade mosaic tiles on the floor, the wooden surfaces on the walls, the lighting fixtures and the furniture fabrics. In addition, the shade colours of grey, white and blue, as well as the pictures of the Neo-classical era of Greek architecture, complete the puzzle.

1. Open kitchen
2. Dining area

Ground Floor Plan

Dining area on the first floor brings outdoor scene inside through green plantings implanted in, which also compliments the charming scenery outside and creates a soothing atmosphere for diners. The lighting fixtures dangle from the ceiling and the cable lines serve as decorative elements.

1. Lounge area
2. Dining area
3. Toilet
4. Outdoor dining

First Floor Plan

NAMUS Buffet Restaurant

Completion date: 2011
Location: Gyeonggi, Bundang, Korea
Designer: Kim Chiho/Chiho&Partners
Photos: Indiphos
Area: 980m²
Material: (Floor)Tile, Carpet ; (Walls)Wood louvre panel,
Special paint,Metal fabric; (Ceiling) Special paint

Continuity of geometric structure makes potential space-esthetics by showing various compositions. This project is extracted from a multiple sequence of progressively flattened geometric elements characterised by "continuity and rhythm" blowing through the space, put on the uniform rules.

The restaurant consists of a main hall in centre, 3 more halls and 6 rooms with a unique concept. Using natural materials like stone, wood and steel makes the restaurant environmentally friendly. At the same time it is emphasised its warmth, elegance, colour and texture of the materials.

Centred on a communal table, Kikoski's channeled Lloyd Wright's iconic spiraling white design from 1959 in the nearly all-white 1,600-square-foot-space.

A reasonable lighting plan associated with six different pastel coloured rooms creates a stable illumination and light lines and it makes a comfortable dining environment.

1. Hall
2. Japanese kitchen
3. Cool kitchen
4. VIP room

Floor Plan

The open-kitchen resides in the main hall, as a central stage where the chefs are busy performing their cooking technique. The sculpture hanging from the ceiling in a main hall reminds of the future metropolis image. It is also an icon of the whole space with the symbolism motivated by geometric nature.

The design concept is reliable and energetic features of absolute beauty in a space. Highlighted lines are constitutive elements that separate finishing materials vertically. Horizontal lines are applied to the element that separates the space and makes a path. The dining areas are of different styles but there is a common connection in colour and material selection.

Private rooms provide an intimate dining experience where diners can enjoy their nice meal in a tranquil as well as cozy space. More attention is paid to the lighting fixtures.

ZOZOBRA Noodle Bar

Completion date: 2011
Location: Israel
Architects: Alon Baranowitz and Irene
Kronenberg; www.bkarc.com
Client: Ben Rothschild in partnership with chef
Avi Conforty
Photos: Amit Geron
Area: 450m²

ZOZOBRA is not a romantic space. It is an edgy space, ecstatic and cool.

On the outside, the designers introduced "ZOZOBRA PARK", a linear "hilly" play of topography flanking the restaurant where restless kids can play while their parents enjoy a quiet moment. Planted amongst these hills are two vertical screens communicating ZOZOBRA's world to the street.

ZOZOBRA offers a dynamic eating experience through a fast service supported by an energetic cool staff geared with wireless pads, a sizzling state of the art open kitchen, and a local service code which states: "Whichever dish is ready, we serve to the table. No firsts, no mains…"

Sections

All of these features encourage guests to react to the space and to each other. Technology is a key feature in our lives and so does ZOZOBRA. It reacts to that reality and embraces it.

The open kitchen is a key element of the layout scheme. It is a powerful feature; the heart and soul of ZOZOBRA.

The designers did not settle for just exposing it, they needed to radiate out the energies which burst within its counter tops, works and grills.

A three-dimensional origami structure folds around the kitchen, wrapping up its space like a white cloud, creating a sort of a tempest "dancing" around the kitchen. While looking into the kitchen, not only guests would see 12 people "in battle", but also, a strong movement and vitality played by the architecture to compliment it.

Ground Floor Plan

Up with the cloud to the gallery level is where the public toilets are located.

The highly reflective black membrane finish of the restaurant ceiling amplifies and reflects anything that happens on the floor.

1. Service kitchen
2. Preparation kitchen
3. Dinning
4. Bar
5. Dish washing area
6. Restrooms
7. Food&beverage storage
8. Take away order room
9. Pasta prep area
10. Mechanical room
11. Offices
12. Staff changing room
13. General storage
14. Men's restroom
15. Women's restroom

First Floor Plan

Section

At **ZOZOBRA**, private territory is blurred and replaced by a chance for social interaction. The ambiance of the venue varies as the day progresses thanks to the ever-changing LED lighting schemes and the video art, specially directed for the project, shooting the inner world of **ZOZOBRA** on the walls.

Kinugawa

Completion date: 2012
Location: Paris, France
Designer: Gilles & Boissier
Photos: Matthieu Salvaing

Design Brief
Helping the renowned restaurant "Kinugawa" – long acknowledged as the Parisian hub of Japanese gourmet cuisine – to further its reputation by creating a space that lends itself to the classic Japanese culinary experience, with echoes of Japanese "Zen" lifestyle. The starting concept was to find a way to combine Japanese culture with French social etiquette and "joie de vivre". Gilles & Boissier were chosen by the restaurant owner to rise to the challenge of creating a space which emanates a jovial & complaisant atmosphere as experienced in a traditional Parisian "brasserie" in an overtly Japanese context.

Design Challenge

The challenge for Gilles & Boissier was bring to life a design which embodies both the traditional & contemporary soul of Japan. The two-sided nature of the Japanese culture is inspired and embodied in Japan's two major cities – Tokyo & Kyoto. The contemporary aspect of the design takes its influence directly from daring & dynamic Tokyo; the traditional aspects explore the tenets of the Zen aesthetic, referring to contemplative & calm Kyoto. The most testing aspect of the project was the amalgamation of both contemporary & traditional Japanese culture with a French touch.

Open Kitchen

Dinging Area

The open-kitchen is considered as the focal point of the restaurant, which creates a stage effect for diners to enjoy the chef's performance while eating their nice meal.

Wooden openwork pillared partitions are used throughout the space and are reflected along the mirrored staircase wall, which plays on a theme of mixing light and shadow as found within Japanese theatre.

The first floor serves as the "workshop". In this large, more traditional space people find an eclectic combination of raw materials used to give depth and texture to the walls. Ranging from darkened cedar wood, scorched stone-work & raw leather seating, such use of natural materials is elementary to all G& B design projects. The floor is dominated by an elegant & stylish mottled-red floor-rug, alluding to the geishas of antiquity.

An impressive 6m high wall mural – the original work of artist Alix Waline – invokes the motion & movement of water and transports people to the Japanese water gardens as depicted in traditional Japanese embossed art. The size and presence of this piece is juxtaposed with its subtle colours and "Zen" undertones in accordance with the overall "Tokyo & Kyoto/ Modern & Classic" design theme.

Vintaged Restaurant at Hilton Brisbane

Completion date: 2011
Location: Brisbane, Australia
Designer: Landini Associates Pty Ltd
Photos: Trevor Mein – Mein Photography
Area: 566m² (restaurant & kitchen) + 200m² (bar)

In 1985 the world famous Modernist architect Harry Seidler completed the only hotel he was ever commissioned to design. Twenty-five years later Landini Associates have remodeled its restaurant and bar. Intended in part as "homage" to the great man Landini took their cues from the building's splendid grandeur and have designed a classic space with a timeless simplicity.

1. Existing counter
2. Existing piano
3. Existing banquette seating
   to remain
4. Bar
5. Existing banquette seating
   to remain
6. Mirror
7. Glazing
8. Mobile unit
9. Buffet
10. Grill
11. Cheese table
12. Cold wall
13. Prep cooking
14. Dry age case
15. Bar storage
16. Bar cool room
17. Office
18. Lift
19. Relocated cool room
20. Maitre d'
21. Wine Table
22. Wine Room
23. Female WC
24. Male WC
25. Private dining room
26. Storage
27. Waiter Station
28. Temporary wall & doors
    to be installed

Floor Plan

The restaurant is located on a raised platform to separate it from the surrounding reception and public spaces. It is entered by a wide stair leading from its bar which sits under the twenty-five floor atrium.

On entering one is greeted by the Maître D who operates from a stainless steel drum, framed by the backdrop of the restaurant's glazed wine room. To the right is an open kitchen and grill, to the left the main dining room. A chef's table sits in front of the open cooking area, which is constructed entirely in black stone to highlight both the aging beef and the chefs who prepare it.

In front of the wine room is a long table for groups and wine tasting classes. These dark finishes extend the length of the dining room and public corridor along which it runs. Mirrors dress this public space and are fitted with vertical lights for added glamour.

Dark leather custom designed banquettes, walnut and ebony chairs and tables allow the modernist red lounges to complement the otherwise white interior of the hotel.

Artwork was specially commissioned but also found in drawings unearthed from Seidler's studio and then enlarged and placed behind the monochrome reception.

1. Buffet
2. Open grill
3. Buffet
4. Coffee pass
5. Kitchen

1. Entry
2. Maitre d' Behind
6. Waiting area behind
4. Wine table
5. Wine room
6. Private dining room
7. WC

1. To back of house
2. Open kitchen behind
3. Glazing
4. Maitre d'
5. Entry
6. Glazing
7. Corridor

1. Victoria room
2. Banquette seating
3. Hotel lobby

1. Victoria room
2. Storage
3. Private dining room
4. Wine room
5. Maitre d'
6. Entry
7. Hotel Lobby

Lluçanès Restaurant in Barcelona

Location: Barcelona, Spain
Designer: Josep Ferrando
Photos: Adria Goula
Area: 500m^2

The programme is divided between the two floors, on the ground floor a more informal, and at the top, a Michelin Star restaurant.

The architectural solutions to distribute the programme are both light and acoustic response of the space. The lamp is solved by a steel plate painted white and perforated according to a mosaic that remembers your settings so characteristic of the neighbourhood where the restaurant is situated. Behind the plate, perforated fabric absorbs while acoustically diffuses light.

The upper and lower position of the lights generate a dialogue between the static (the project) and dynamic (the user): adjust light intensity when you are standing (dynamic) and light in darkness when you sit (static).

The lower fixture gives lightness and buoyancy to the element aspect lamp located inside the kitchen and bathrooms.

Model

125

This ground floor space as a continuum of the square, with a large opening in front and a continuous concrete floor, becomes a door space between public and market. The layout creates two working parties on both sides of the flow of people: one open, where the layout of the kitchens in perpendicular promotes cooking show, and one closed to the dirty area with access from the outside service. Lighting along the length of the place reinforces the idea of continuity, turning the square into a restaurant and the restaurant plaza.

The walls painted black background reinforce the sense of infinity from the public space. On the ground floor facing a large blackboard acts black, while the facing first floor fragments to locate the necessary furniture, leaves two large openings that give visual continuity to the deck in the double-height space. The furniture is situated opposite the skylights to increase light coming downstairs.

The first floor is achieved by a great cabinet space; positioned asymmetrically in the room, it creates four places between the perimeter of the façades and to which never touches, so that the container and metal beams have continuity. The floor, with references to aerial photographs of fields, indicating the importance of raw material at a restaurant in this category, while carpets generates three intensities of gray that individualise each table space, avoiding the feeling of great dining room.

Gray tones on the first floor are repeated in the dress of the tables, as if they were part of the floor, while ground floor provides a single colour, orange, which qualifies the different types of premises. This colour is always at the height of the sight of the person sitting on chairs, stools, aprons. The materiality of the proposal seeks to maintain the industrial character of the market, using steel plates and concrete.

The white wall-lamp at an altitude of just 2.8m, from which the black takes away space for installation.

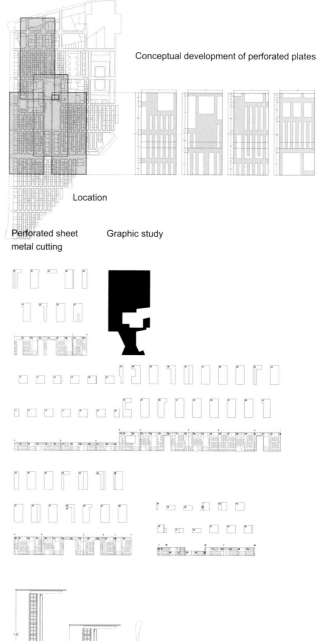

Conceptual development of perforated plates

Location

Perforated sheet metal cutting

Graphic study

Bar type section(1/20)

1. Kitchen
2. Refrigerating chamber
3. Preparation area
4. Cleaning area
5. Café area
6. Women's restroom
7. Men's restroom
8. Toilet for handicaps
9. VIP room
10. Dining room

1. Cleaning area
2. Kitchen
3. Dining room
4. Refrigerating chamber
5. Stock
6. Machinery
7. Control area
8. Reception material
9. Service access
10. Terrace

Site Plan

Hilton Pattaya – Restaurants, Lobby & Bar and Linkage Spaces

Completion date: 2010
Location: Pattaya, Thailand
Designer: Waraphan Watanakaroon
Photos: Wison Tungthunya
Area: Lobby and "Drift" Bar: 1,650m²; "Edge" Restaurant: 1,200m²; "Flare" Fine Dining: 205m²

Waraphan Watanakaroon is responsible for interior design of various common areas for Hilton Pattaya Hotel which includes the Ground Floor Lobby, the Main Lobby on the 16th floor, "Drift" Bar, "Edge" Restaurant, "Flare" Fine Dining, and various common area and linkage spaces within the building. The hotel is part of a larger multi-used complex located in the heart of Pattaya, overlooking the Pattaya beach.

1. Open kitchen
2. Dining area

Edge Floor Plan

0 1 2   5   10

"Edge" Restaurant

A restaurant serving international food with multiple large open kitchens is situated on the 13th floor facing the ocean view. Its main spatial organisation strategy is to open up the ocean view to the guests at its maximum to take advantage of the view from its prime location. The space is stretched linearly along the glass wall facing the sea with an almost 8 metre-high ceiling. The indoor seating area is organised into two tiers where the floor towards the back is higher up to ensure a good view over the front part. The outdoor terrace with its impressive panoramic view in the front lets the ocean vista flows uninterruptedly to the inside by arranging its floor plate a step lower.

Away from the busy street down below, the restaurant provides a calm, relaxing and comfortable atmosphere. An airy space with the use of natural materials and light colours allow the guests to set back and relax. The open kitchen area is accentuated with special material treatment as a focal point of the interior space.

The visual elements in the space are loose reminiscent of an underwater landscape – sea fan and translucent luminous ocean creatures. The interior surfaces are almost transformed from their original materiality into thin gorgonian membranes wrapping the space. Clusters of glowing organic-shape lamps suspended randomly in mid-air with varying sizes and colours scatter throughout the space. Hidden in the restaurant restroom, maneuvering through its interior space, one cannot resist thinking of the space in between the seabed fauna.

As a focal point of the interior space, open kitchen is accentuated with special material treatment

Layerings of crystal, coloured sheer cloth, and wired-sculptured frame compose the lamp that gives extraordinary shadow to the interior space

Natural material and light colour with natural sunlight gives a relaxing feel to the overall area

A cluster of glowing organic-shape light fixtures with crisscrossing-wooden membrane surface backdrop

View of the interior space with clusters of suspended lamps varying in sizes and colours

Crisscrossing slat wall facing the casual dining space below
marks an entrance to the fine dining

Dining table with wine cellar background

Translucent volume of sheer fabric as a privacy screening yet connecting the spaces at the same time

0 1 2   5   10

Floor Plan

"Flare" Fine Dining

An upscale luxury fine dining serving grill is located on a 14th floor. Privacy and exclusivity for the guests play an important role in the project. The design explores a mediating means of space demarcation between pockets of private dining area. By occupying an intermediary space between spaces with a translucent volume of sheer fabric, the effect results in an elegant, mystifying atmosphere, engaging and disengaging different spaces at the same time.

A deep colour palette gives an even further perplexing depth. A slight up-light to the volume of sheer fabric and the glowing light at the edge of the fabric accentuated the lighting in the space. The glitter of crystal lamps and chandeliers sparks and enriches the depth of the space.

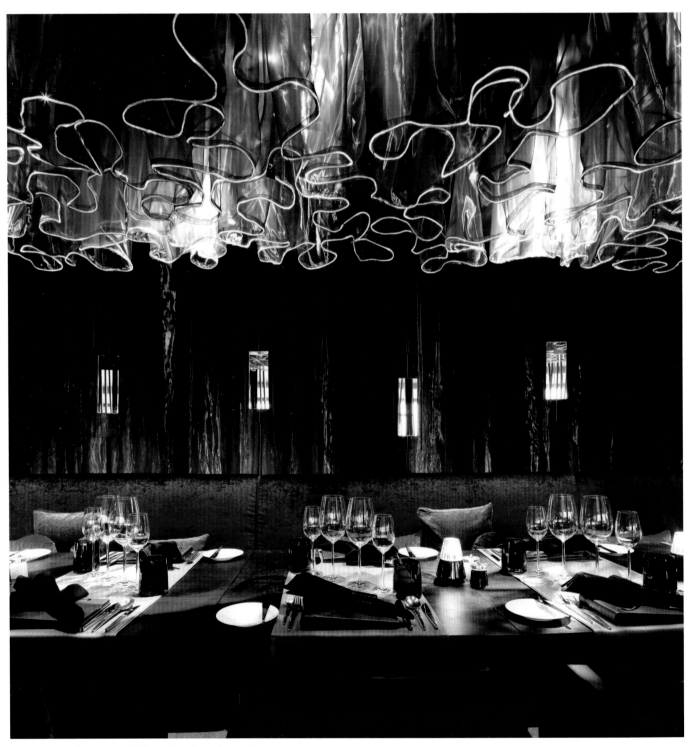

Glittering elements within a deep interior colour

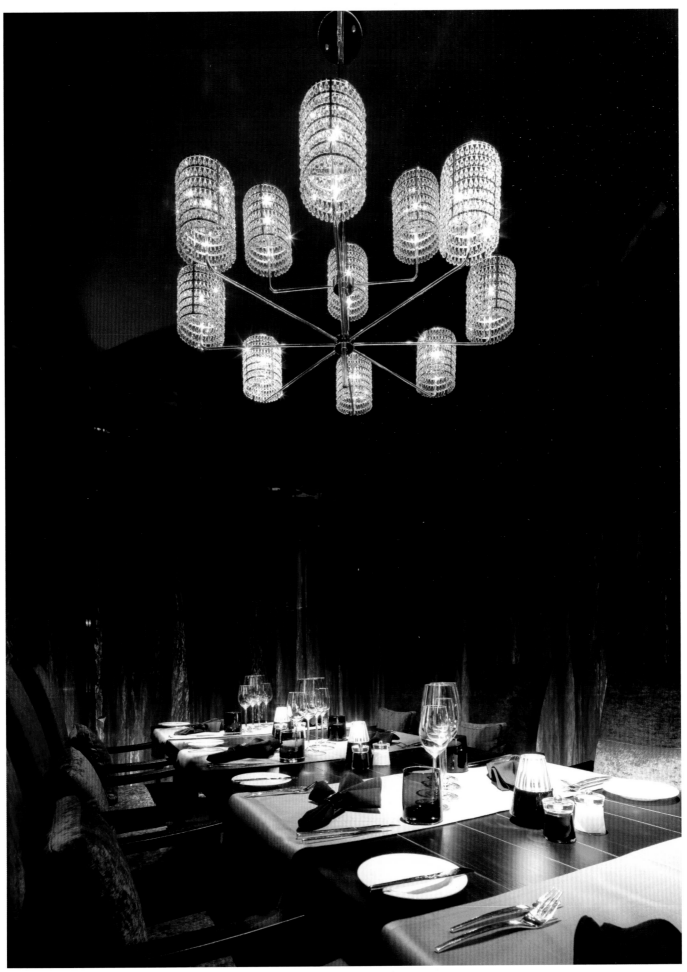

Private dining space

Assaggio Trattoria Italiana

Completion date: 2011
Location: Hong Kong, China
Designer: David Tsui, Suzanne Chong
Photos: Graham Uden
Area: 800m²

HASSELL was appointed by the Miramar Group to provide interior design consultancy for the Assaggio Trattoria Italiana Restaurant in Hong Kong, China. Assaggio Trattoria Italiana Restaurant is located on the fifth floor, inside the Hong Kong Arts Centre in Wanchai, adjacent to the Academy of Performing Art.

The restaurant has been well received by the customers and the general public since its opening in March 2011, and the completion of this project has created a great business relationship between HASSELL and the Miramar Group.

Sustainability
HASSELL's sustainable design approach is "Design with Nature". In order to introduce a green, natural, fresh and lively dining experience to the restaurant's dining guests, the design team used natural timber flooring, a recycled timber slab for the bar counter, old display cabinets as well as an herb garden outside.

1. M&E service
2. PIZZA bar
3. AHU room
4. Light well
5. Kitchen
6. VIP room

Floor Plan

Given its interesting location, the design concept of the restaurant is based on an artistic theatrical performance. Assaggio means "taste" and "little bites" in Italian language. The design concept aims to create a "dining stage" for the diners. The interior design is a deliberate attempt to make the venue look like a stage setting of a cosy Italian grocery store – and every paying customer in the restaurant is also seen as a part of the performance which tells a story about dining. The idea is to bring home a hearty Italian affair that transport diners to the friendly streets of Italy.

Deep wood hues make for a soothing dining scene and Italy is represented through vibrant art pieces fixed over rustic stone finishes. In addition, HASSELL proposed the idea of a pizza and pasta bar at the entrance of the restaurant to attract diners' attention upon their arrival and lead them to move to the Al Fresco area, which has a stunning view of the Victoria Harbour.

Sugarcane

Completion date: 2010
Location: Miami, USA
Designer: Cetra Ruddy
Photos: Andrew Meade
Area: 446m²

Springing from restaurateur SushiSamba's unique blend of Japanese, Brazilian, and Peruvian cuisine, music, and design, Sugarcane raw bar grill is a new tapas-style restaurant located in Miami's newly developing Design District. The restaurant/ lounge features an 80m² indoor/outdoor bar and three distinct kitchens: robata, hot and raw bar. The spirited design is evocative of the Brasilian favela and features organic textures, salvaged ironwork, aged wood floors, reclaimed shutters, vintage "found objects", graffiti art and modern design, creating a sense of authenticity and age. Custom-designed banquettes, eclectic combinations of tables and chairs, hand-painted Moroccan tiles, antique mirrors and vintage fans create a comfortable yet festive atmosphere.

The signature robata bar showcases the high flame cooking activity with bar seating for patrons to watch the chef at work. Both the indoor/outdoor and robata bars create a sense of drama and energy, allowing patrons to view each other and encouraging interaction.

Notable elements include the garden, robata bar and indoor/outdoor bar. The garden, hidden from the street by a hedge, continues the worldly experience through antique patio furniture, tropical plants, full height specimen trees and vines which cover the walls and window lattice ironwork. The indoor/outdoor was custom-designed with sliding glass doors that penetrate the centre of the bar, slipping behind a back-lit wall displaying the unique selection of sakes, tequilas and liquors.

1. Lounge
2. Robarta bar
3. Kitchen
4. Raw bar
5. Indoor/outdoor bar

Floor Plan

Sugarcane's variety of forms, styles and colours create a casual environment and communal experience that compliments the restaurant's initiative: for guests to kick back, eat well and stay awhile.

The favela design immediately immerses guests in an authentic and transformational experience of tropical culture and history. Multiple layers of multi-coloured paint create an aged patina which is echoed by the distressed furniture and finishes. The result is an atmosphere that is rich in character, embracing and timeless.

Symphony's

Completion date: 2009
Location: Amsterdam, The Netherlands
Designer: D/DOCK
Photos: Foppe Peter Schut
Area: 950m^2

With its multi-functional restaurant concept on Amsterdam's Southern Axis (Zuidas), Symphony's is meeting the huge demand from the many professionals in the area for a restaurant with an atmosphere and ambiance that holds its own with restaurants in the city centre. In cooperation with Vijverborgh – which developed the horeca concept – D/DOCK was responsible for the design and layout of Symphony's. A versatile restaurant that is a cross between a company restaurant and an establishment that is open to the public.

1. Terrace
2. Entrance
3. Show kitchen box
4. Bar/ coffee bar

Ground Floor Plan

In the heart of the restaurant, there is a show kitchen in which the chefs cook in full view of the guests, creating a feeling of authenticity, freshness and dependability.

The multi-functionality of Symphony's, which is embedded in the layout and design of the concept, makes it an attractive port of call throughout the day for company employees and people from the surrounding offices. The same space where coffee and breakfast are served early in the mornings transforms into a popular cocktail bar in the evenings.

Symphony's has been turned into a comfortable and fashionable restaurant with a characteristic layout based on the "Techno India" theme. The unusual use of colour and the recurring paisley pattern set the restaurant from its options for use.

De Gusto

Completion date: 2009
Location: Ravenna, Italy
Designer: Arch. Camilla Lapucci & Lapo Bianchi Luci
Photos: Pietro Savorelli
Area: 300m²

De Gusto can be defined an "Italian pasta University", it is a tasting hall located inside Surgital industrial complex in Lavezzola (RA), leading company in deep frozen pasta exportation.

The hall is a culinary laboratory and it represents the heart of the "Research & Development" department. It is really impor-

tant because it is the kitchen where Surgital can connect with its customer and promote its work.

The opening party was directed by the international chef Gianfranco Vissani and many public officers were invited to the event. A special menu was created and cooked inside De Gusto kitchen, pasta was obviously the main element. The menu was richly completed with "Divine Creazioni", the excellent fine line.

The idea of De Gusto rises up from the necessity of creating a representative room as a memorable end of the visiting path of the company. Everyone can observe excellent chefs cooking.

"Every week we host restaurant owners and usually we offer tasting samples of our product at the end of the visit" says Elena Bacchini – Surgital Marketing Director – "we usually contact external famous chef to create culinary experimental events".

Floor Plan

1. Entrance hall
2. Store
3. Sink and WC
4. Office
5. Open kitchen
6. Dining area

1. Roof structure
2. Steel structure
3. Cross beam
4. Plasterboard panel for communication
5. Light linear diffuser hidden into plasterboard ceiling
6. Light linear diffuser on railed metallic profile
7. Linear air vent
8. Recessed spotlight
9. Wood portal
10. Plasterboard structure
11. Railed spotlight

0   0.5   1 m

Ceiling detail

A technologic heart of professional devices is the real heart of the kitchen, covered with calacatta marble, the one traditionally used as table to prepare hand-made pasta. Next to it there is a 15m long table with thirty stools to watch the preparation from the first line.

Main characters of De Gusto are materials and textures. Grey concrete floor, porous brushed oak wood furniture, calacatta marble veins and Japanese barely wall paper create a domestic and familiar atmosphere that exalt pure, essential volumes.

Nature and Technology are strictly connected: a vertical garden goes with visitors along entrance stairs and inside all fine senses are stimulated.

The interior design is functional, rigorous but minimal and simple. Each one can easily individuate all functions and enjoy them naturally. The open space is divided into a technologic interactive kitchen and in a sort of big lecture hall. Couples of long wooden tables, where about eight people can take a sit, are placed each one on a step of a huge stair in front of the kitchen. Visitors can observe excellent chefs cooking and then taste their creation prepared with Surgital product.

De Gusto confirms the high quality of "Made in Italy", as Surgital does it constantly exporting its products all over the world. The great result is due to the ability of architects C+L Studio to mix traditional culinary elements, proposed in an upgraded contemporary layout, and technologic devices, audio and video system.

Karls Kitchen

Completion date: 2010
Location: Stuttgart, Germany
Client: E. Breuninger GmbH & Co.
Designer: Concrete Architectural Associates
Project team: Rob Wagemans
        Melanie Kn ü wer
        Charlotte Key
        Erik van Dillen
        Sofie Ruytenberg (graphic design)
Photos: Ewout Huibers
Area: 1,000m²
Seats: 400

Karls Kitchen is the new restaurant of luxury department store Breuninger in Stuttgart.

The kitchen is the free-flow restaurant's central element. The entrance to the restaurant is characterised by large glass fridges with fresh products that also function as a display window.

Materials:
Floor: The entire restaurant is fitted with smooth, oak floors, with a different finish for each seating area (white, grey and black).
· Kitchen: Terrazzo tiles (colour custom-made), 60x60cm
· Toilets: Floor tiles Mosa, beige and brown, 15x60cm
Ceiling: The entire restaurant is fitted with a white acoustic plasterboard ceiling, except the more intimate areas have a dark ceiling. The lounge is fitted with a dark wood vertical panel ceiling; the kitchens have a black metal ceiling and the private kitchen has its ceiling painted black.

Wall: Custom-made wallpaper, Concrete's design produced by Berlintapete.
Interior: Custom-made furnishings, such as the "Stammtisch", the children's corner, the sofas and the tables, were designed by Concrete and produced by Van Bergh, interior builder.
Lighting: The green hanging lamps in the modern section were specially designed by Concrete and produced by Baulmann.
In the lounge area, the hanging lamp by Raimond van Moooi and the Base standard lamp from Tom Dixon create the intimate atmosphere.
The porcelain lamps above the "Stammtisch" come from a Dutch ceramics studio.
In the kitchen section and the walking areas, spotlights with close lighting bundles provide a theatrical effect.
Furniture: There is a choice of various chairs for each guest. Nearly all the tables and chairs have something classical with a

Nearly all the tables and chairs have something classical with a modern interpretation. The chair and the InOut bar stool from Gervasoni have a very simple form but are made of aluminium. The Morph van Zeitraum chair in the modern seating area is made of walnut.
The tables and AVL benches in the traditional section are from Moooi.
The Ray black leather lounge chairs and the DLM metal tables are from Hay. The outdoor furniture from the Tio series is from Massproduction.

THE KITCHENS

The guest's initial experience is on coming in, walking through the kitchens, barely separated from the preparation of fresh products by a large glass wall.

To the left you can see exclusive sandwiches, fresh salads and homemade desserts being prepared. On the right you can take a peek into the warm kitchens, where traditional local classics, Asian and European specialities are prepared. The dishes, which change daily, are presented on a row of screens above the two kitchen counters.

The materials used reference the classic kitchen of grandma's time: white tiles, black natural stone in combination with a terrazzo floor. The modern design in combination with new materials such as glass and stainless steel create a modern design with a link to the classic kitchen.

THE BAR

Opposite the kitchens is the bar, a free-standing element between the free-flow restaurant and the seating area. The bar's function is two-fold: on the kitchen side, cakes and pastries are made in-store; fresh juices and beverages are offered.

The bar adjacent to the lounge area tempts one to sit at the bar and enjoy a nice glass of wine, a glass of local beer or one of the coffee specialities.

The materials used for the bar create a connection between the restaurants and the kitchens. The bar is made of wooden tiles in the same dimensions as the kitchen tiles, on top of which is a black natural stone surface, creating a warm appearance and being functional at the same time.

1. Warm kitchen (80m^2)
2. Cold kitchen (50m^2)
3. Bar (55m^2)
4. Traditional restaurant (100m^2)
5. Contemporary restaurant (195m^2)
6. Private kitchen (43m^2)
7. Dishwashing area (32m^2)

Floor Plan

The Lounge

The Lounge area in the middle of the space is directly adjacent to the bar. The lounge has a relaxed atmosphere with low lounge chairs and an extra long black leather sofa. In the middle a hanging fireplace provides an intimate feel. The lounge-character is reinforced by a lowered black vertical strip ceiling and a dark-grey wooden floor.

The lounge is linked directly to the terrace by means of the vertical panel ceiling which runs from inside to outside. The outside panels also serve as an awning.

The terrace's wooden floor is continued inside, forming a long table along the façade, allowing one to enjoy the view of Stuttgart from indoors as well.

THE RESTAURANT

The restaurant is divided into 3 different seating areas, each with its own identity and character. First of all there is the traditional seating area, which refers to Breuninger's history and the traditions within the department store, as well as in Stuttgart. The modern seating area represents the Stuttgart of today, and the Lounge is the refuge and, at the same time, the connection between the modern and the traditional seating areas.

An overarching element connecting the spaces to one another is one long wall with graphic wallpaper. Where walls are interrupted by glass panels or doors, the glass is decorated with the same print, but transparent, thereby maintaining the overall image.

The Traditional Restaurant

The traditional part is a modern interpretation of an original "Bierstube". The central element here is the "Stammtisch" (table for the regulars). This is one big table from which pieces have been cut for the sofas. The solid-oak top contrasts with the white legs, which are made of Corian. In total the table provides seating space for 34 people. In the middle of the table there is, just like in the modern section, a high cabinet up to the ceiling.

This cabinet is filled with coloured red products such as kitchenware and local souvenirs. The red recurs in a number of chairs, which provide a hint of colour between the white furniture.

Above each table hang two lamps. These resemble a classic embroidered lampshade from grandma's time. What is unique about the lamps is that they are made of white porcelain with a red iron cable. It thereby ties in with the concept of an old-fashioned product with a contemporary twist.

The white bare oak floors of the traditional section reinforce the light atmosphere. The children's play corner is right next to the traditional seating area. It is a kind of open box made of the same white wood as the floor. Red cushions, beanbags and stickers with red animals on the glass side walls create a playful touch.

There is a dedicated parking place for pushchairs with a parking meter.

The Modern Restaurant

The modern seating area is defined by contemporary materials, such as Corian, light-coloured leather, chrome in combination with dark wood.

The central element is a furniture piece in the middle of the room. It comprises long sofas with light leather upholstery connected by a high cabinet. In this cabinet there are cooking utensils in silver and chrome which reflect towards the modern character.

The dark wooden floor creates a subtle contrast with the light furniture.

The custom-made hanging lamps, with the different dimensions and shades of green, provide a playful touch.

Private Kitchen

Alongside the three seating areas there is the restaurant's

private kitchen, which can be closed off by means of a sliding glass door. The room has its own free-standing cooker and can be used for cooking workshops, parties, presentations or business meetings. The materials, such as the white tiles and the kitchenware along the walls, partly come from the kitchen. The dark wooden floor and a black ceiling create an intimate, informal atmosphere.

The River Café

Completion date: 2008
Location: London, UK
Designer: Stuart Forbes Associates / Stuart Forbes and Richard Rogers
Photos: Grant Smith
Area: 468m²

The River Café, one of London's most celebrated restaurants, re-opened its doors on 6 October 2008 after a £2 million re-design. Following a fire in April 2008, co-owners Ruth Rogers and Rose Gray commissioned Stuart Forbes Associates to re-design the space with a new open kitchen, private dining room and cocktail bar.

Since the re-launch, the restaurant has enjoyed the acclaim of the world's food critiques and architectural press and continues to be one of the most influential food establishments.

1. Main entrance
2. Bar
3. Coat room
4. Wine storage
5. Restaurant
6. Terrace
7. Garden
8. Desserts
9. Cold foods
10. Kitchen
11. Wash up
12. Private dining
13. Cheese store
14. Staff changing
15. Deliveries entrance

Floor Plan

Significant additions include a kitchen table within the working kitchen zone and a glass enclosed cheese room based on a classic Italian design. The kitchen is open to public view, enabling diners to observe the chefs in action.

Another notable addition is a new wood burning oven dominating the dining room and kitchen. Manufactured by the Italian firm of Valoriani, this type of oven, made in Reggello in the hills of Tuscany 25km southeast of Florence, is key to the preparation of the The River Café's many dishes.

The reception desk and "pass" have been constructed in vivid yellow "Corian" and dramatically top-lit. This new area is located next to The River Café bar which has been adapted and enhanced with a new back-lit bottle display. Behind the scenes, the bathrooms have been re-planned and reconstructed with fluorescent primary colours and significantly increased space.

Section A

Front elevation

Back elevation

Oven Design

Section A
1. All white
2. Yellow
3. Open access to back of equipment
4. Power sockets

Plan 1

Plan 2

Plan 3

Plan 1
1. Brackets and plates sizes
2. Curved to stop here at 80mm from front edge. Then to become straight to achieve a clear front edge

Plan 2
1. Φ75mm cut out to allow of cables connection. Provide edge detail

Plan 3
1. Pull out tray for keyboard
2. 515mm equal on both sides

Detail section
1. Curved Top to allow for lighting feature Hout Tek to liason with lighting consultant for appropriate spacing connection details and transformers location on the desk
2. S/S Posts 50x8mm to connect Curved Top with Bottom Foot
3. 25mm Upstand with 20mm rounded junction to counter top

Detail section

Plan 4

Plan 3

Plan 2

Section A

Plan 1

Front elevation

Back elevation

Section A
1. Lighting feature
2. Curved top area
3. Fixing Plate between Vertical S/S Post and underside of Curved Top

Front elevation
1. S/S Posts 50x8mm to connect Curved Top with Bottom Foot
2. "Corian" or similar approved
   Colour: Blue to be confirmed by sample provided by Hout Tek

3. Φ50mm St.Steel 304 Tubular Footrail on St.Steel Bracket
4. Φ50mm S/S Posts Legs on Φ100mm Stability Plate. Fixed to desk underside and connected to vertical posts as required

Back elevation
1. "Corian" or similar approved
2. Colour: Blue to be confirmed by sample provided by Hout Tek

Detail A, Detail B, Typical frame elevation

Detail A
1. Optional additional pan shelf
2. Shelf cavity with recessed lighting
3. Flush mounted S/S double
electrical socket facing inward
towards the pre surface

Detail B
1. Optional additional pan shelf
2. Shelf cavity with reccssed lighting
3. Shelf cavity with reccssed lighting
4. Flush mounted S/S double
electrical socket facing inward
towards the pre surface

Typical frame elevation
1. Work surface
2. 20mm solid bar
3. Cut out for 2x electrical plug socket

General note
All fabricated steel to be S/S Grade 316
Brushed finish to match worktops
All through bolts to be countersunk hexagon socket machine screws
Cut plate steel to bolt onto 60x30mm box section frame fixed to base table
All steel sizes shown are indicative and must be verified by the contractor

There are dining areas of different styles in the restaurants, which add the flexibility and diversity of the interior and provide more choice for diners.

Note
The dimensions shown on the original square plate and eye are taken from the existing brackets in the River Café. The original glass specification is 10mm toughened monolithic sheets. In the event that this specification changes to a laminated panel, the unit weight must be taken into account when proof checking the bolt fixings and bracket back to the structural soffit.
The bolt fixings to the structural soffit are drilled and tapped into the flange of the steel beams of the original building fabric.
The fixing method shown is for illustrative purposes as "design intent" and must be verified by a structural engineer.
All component pieces are fabricated in stainless steel.

Component pieces

Proposed bracket

Assembly of glass panel to bracket and structural soffit

1. Panel shown vertical
2. Laminated glass panel
3. Structural soffit
4. Acoustic quilt
5. S/S weld mesh ceiling panel
6. Range of panel movement

Bar Brasserie Restaurant Fitch & Shui

Completion date: 2011
Location: Amsterdam, The Netherlands
Designer: D/DOCK
Photos: Ronald Nieuwendijk
Area: 1,400m²

Located in the Amsterdam WTC building, the Fitch & Shui restaurant is the eye catcher from the front side of the building. The big glass façade gives a passers-by free view inside on the long bar and the cozy seating at the window. The elon-gated space asked for a big gesture like the bar to define the space. The setup of the bar also symbolises its use: starting with breakfast, fresh juice, sandwiches for lunch, cocktails at the bar and a big "wine painting" at the end.

Together with the hanging meat and other fresh products on and behind the bar, the bar is made to be a "food theatre", where honest products are sold by experience, completely in line with the Fitch & Shui concept.

Section

1. Terrace
2. Bar
3. Kitchen
4. Dining area
5. Entrance

Floor Plan

The self-service restaurant has a free-flow setup and has seating for 300 people. The interior provides different seating typologies: high, low, half-high, bench, chair and stool. These variations in seating possibilities divide the space in areas and the different modules give protection in the big open space, in a simple cost effective way.

Along the windows a variety of furniture like big couches, fauteuil's, stools, big lamps and several mood and styling elements are set up in a playful way. The space as a whole breaths a warm cosmopolitan ambiance with an old-skool twist.

The walls are cover with a graphic illustration of herbs, specially designed for Fitch & Shui, by D/DOCK. In leather-upholstered couches, black or wooden tables and spherical lamps are placed throughout the space, enhancing the feeling or the different protected modules. All these elements give the self-service restaurant a simplistic modern classic appearance, with an industrial touch.

FRESH CUTT

Completion date: 2009
Location: Sherman Oaks, USA
Designer: AkarStudios
Photos: Randall Michelson
Area: 223m²

Featuring a dramatically lit open kitchen and serving counter, the quick-service Mediterranean concept is a result of a major transformation of a space that previously housed a salad-bar concept. The former venue was completely altered to create a sense of freshness that would appeal to an aspirational audi-ence. With an array of contemporary eco-friendly materials and finishes, the design has been kept clean and simple, with the main counter becoming the focal point. AkarStudios creat-ed a branded identity and graphics programme for the launch-ing of this new concept.

1. Kitchen
2. Exhibition kitchen
3. Prep counter
4. Dining
5. Restroom

Ground Floor Plan

Colourful glass-clad soffit hangs above the main preparation counter

Dining area incorporates seating with tall backs upholstered in a warm rust textured fabric. Above the back, on the recycled wood wall are monitors displaying the preparation methods and ingredients of the menu

Made up of two interconnecting spaces with a high ceiling, the first space is an eating area that has a parallel row of banquet seating along the walls facing an outdoor patio. The second space is the exhibition kitchen – a long cook line whose focal point is the front preparation counter displaying an array of fresh and locally-sourced natural ingredients. A backdrop colour scheme incorporating a combination of beige and taupe shades conjoins the two spatial uses.

Within the dining space, extensive use of recycled stained wood paneling has been made to create a comfortable and warm area for the dining customers. Other defining features include the use of back-painted glass and eye-catching wall graphics specially created for this venue.

Detail of the main counter incorporating recycled wood components

Seating banquette with monitor above

Restaurant signage

Seating wall with recycled wood paneling

Dining seating with wall graphic at rear

188

Looking into the space through the glass door

Fusao Restaurant

Completion date: 2008
Location: Lisbon, Portugal
Designer: Joao Tiago Aguiar
Photos: FG+SG Fotografia De
Arquitectura
Area: 250m²

The programme initially given required the creation of a restaurant exclusively dedicated to Japanese cuisine inside a 5 star hotel, contemporary and innovative. The main concept of the project was to give the purity, quietness and cleanness that usually characterise this type of restaurant but at the same time with a contemporary language and using noble and luxurious materials. In that sense, the designers tried to organise the space in a clear way, and to make people feel they are in a different environment immediately after they get to the entrance.

1. Open kitchen
2. Dining area

Floor Plan

The open-kitchen dining area becomes the focal point of the restaurant: white marble counter corresponds to the concept of simpilicity and boasts elegant theme. Besides, they have also created two winter gardens at the bottom, both in small white river stone, in order to give it a more oriental atmosphere, one of them (by the entrance) being reinforced with the use of big rain forest stone panels (1.4x2.7m size) imported from the Amazonia forest in Brazil.

The space is mainly divided by two great gestures: one is the counter made all in white marble stone, 8cm thick, that cuts the whole space and folds and turns creating different areas for diners to seat and enjoy either the Sushi and Sashimi or the Tepan-Ya-ki; the other is a great loose concrete block lifted from the ground and not touching the ceiling with a stream of light all around both below and on top that closes and opens and has all the private rooms where one can appreciate all the food in a more private, quiet and relaxed environment.

The ceiling was powdered by small little boxes that work as skylights, allowing the natural light to come in from various points as well.

0 0.5 1   3

0 0.5 1   3

0 0.5 1

0 0.5 1

Sections

La Oliva

Completion date: 2012
Location: Tokyo, Japan
Designer: Aiji Inoue, Yuki Kanai/DOYLE COLLECTION CO.,LTD.
Photos: Satoshi Umetsu/Nacasa&Partners
Area: 48m²

Before designing "La Oliva", the client and the designers visited Spain in advance. The concept for this restaurant was "to bring real Spain to Japan."

The project needed a clear concept to integrate all the below factors into one restaurant; for all of the followings are "real Spain" restaurants.

• Restaurants that emphasise bar style culture and history are most familiar throughout Spain.
• Restaurants that have modern appearance, though you can still feel the Spanish atmosphere, are relatively new type of restaurants in Spain.

Considering the construction costs, the designers wanted to make good balance of Japanese people's preference. They used contemporary methods in total and filled with combinations of beautiful town scenery and clusters of Spanish bars.

Inside the restaurant, the designers placed an open kitchen so that the customers will enjoy the live atmosphere of the cooking. And the further away you sit from the open kitchen, the higher your eye level will become. In this way, no matter where you sit, everyone can easily communicate with the staff members in the kitchen.

1. Entrance
2. Outdoor seating
3. Kitchen counter
4. Sofa seating
5. Floor
6. Showcase
7. Toilet
8. Kitchen

Ground Floor Plan

As for the space construction of the façade, the designers set terrace seats in spacious and inconspicuous boundaries with high tables to make people easier to enter the restaurant and to let the people outside know that it's always crowded.

They brought the local impression into shape; for example, bricks and walls for the blackboard, patterned imprinted tiles, and wooden counters that perfectly harmonise.

The designers displayed photographs, which they took in Spain and made it into a monochrome one, on the upper open counter as one of the designs. All the posters in this restaurant were bought from an antique shop in Spain.

Grand Hyatt Macau – Restaurant "MEZZA9"

Completion date: 2009
Location: Macau, China
Designer: Super Potato
Photos: Restaurant "MEZZA9"
Area: 1,260m²

Mezza9 is a restaurant on the second floor of Grand Hyatt Macau Hotel which opened in 2009 as a part of the complex facility project from a hotel and commercial facility called City of Dreams Project.

1. Entrance
2. Private room
3. Chinese kitchen
4. Drink station
5. Terrace
6. Grill kitchen
7. Walk-in cellar
8. Dessert kitchen
9. Japanese kitchen
10. Toilet

Floor Plan

There are several show kitchens at the Asian and Western stations which allows for guests to see the cooking in front. These kitchens are deemed as the focal point of the restaurant, which not only present the mysterious cooking process to diners, but also add vividness to the entire restaurant. Kitchens' design varies in form and function according to the food provided.

The interior is expressed in a modern manner through materials which elaborates naturalism in a strong way such as stones which were cut out from the mountains, timber with natural faces left, and iron with rust. By segregating these materials with usage of floor, wall and counter, the materials do not only become a material for the interior, yet, also elements to construct an art installation space.

Created by cutting-edge Japanese interior design firm Super

Potato, this eclectic, highly textured 292-seat space is defined by giant, roughly hewn stone blocks forming counters and lining walls, as well as an eye-catching array of lattice-patterned metal screens. Besides the main dining room, guests can choose the outdoor terrace, one of four semi-private, Japanese wood-lined booths, or one of two 10- to 12-seat private rooms.

barQue

Completion date: 2011
Location: Athens, Greece
Designer: k–studio
Branding: DGGD, k–studio
Lighting: Halo
Photos: Vangelis Paterakis

The cuisine of barQue revolves around barbecued meats. This was the starting point for the design and the branding concept. In collaboration with DGGD the branding completes the atmosphere by borrowing the font from the tool used to brand meat before hanging, to design the restaurant logo. The "Taste the Fun" neon motto reminds everyone that barbequing is a sociable activity and that the preparation, grilling and eating of good quality meat should be celebrated.

Barbequing is a social activity, so the design opens up the kitchen and allows the choreography of the chefs to become part of the dining experience, with some diners even sitting along the kitchen worktop to eat. A steel grille, reminiscent of a barbeque grill, acts as a false ceiling that accentuates the height and gives the space a dark, masculine weight.

A deep frieze of cut pine blocks, arranged as an abstraction of the traditional butchers chopping table, is suspended above the bar allowing continuity between the interior and exterior dining areas.

The glow of the wood-block frieze combines with varied pieces of wooden furniture and a large, glass-jar chandelier to warm the space, balancing soft, crafted and delicate textures with the rough black steel ceiling and the blaze of the grill from the open kitchen.

1. Open kitchen
2. Dining area

Ground Floor Plan

La Nonna Restaurant

Completion date: 2010
Location: Mexico City, Mexico
Designer: Cherem Serrano
Photos: Jaime Navarro
Area: 275m²

La Nonna is an Italian restaurant located in La Condesa. This project was made in collaboration with DMG architects. The design premise was to liberate the plan so the restaurant could take the most advantage of the 200 square metres local. The restaurant fuses its environment with simplicity.

Sections

The mirror was placed in order to enlarge the space and create a game of light and shadows. The furniture is elegant and simple. At the centre is placed a bar with a pizza stove and a wood counter to sit and enjoy a nice wine.

Incorporating the use of local materials, the floor is made of dark stone and is built unto the sidewalk, while the walls and ceiling are surrounded by red brick with special cutting on top of mirrors.

The services area in a second level connected with the ground floor by an elegant illuminated staircase. While going down to the main level, the architects created a playful mezzanine that catches the eye of the visitor by letting light in and setting a swinging chair, some books and a floor lamp. The ceiling in the stair and main circulations is painted in black in order to emphasise the design of the red bricks placed in the restaurant area.

1. Steel structure
2. LED lamp
3. Brick screen ceiling
4. Screw
5. 6mm mirror
6. Existing block wall
7. Brick screen wall
8. LED recessed lamp

Detail

1. Kitchen and bar
2. Dining area
3. Stairs

Ground floor plan

First floor plan

The illumination is hidden within the bricks and creates a nice rhythm of light that accentuates the architects concern to integrate the architecture with the functional requirements.

Jaffa – Tel Aviv Restaurant

Completion date: 2011
Location: Tel Aviv, Israel
Designer: Alon Baranowitz and Irene Kronenberg
Photos: Amit Geron
Area: 350m²
Award: 3rd Prize at the AIT Award 2012/ Category: Bar and Restaurants

1. Service kitchen
2. Preparation kitchen
3. Dining
4. Dining bar
5. Wine fridge
6. Restrooms
7. Storage

Haim Cohen, widely known as Israel's first celebrity chef, appointed BK Architects for the design of his new restaurant in Tel Aviv: "Jaffa – Tel Aviv".

In Israel many culinary traditions live together. Inspired by their richness, Cohen considers them only as a starting point. With a touch of ingenuity, bearing honesty and subtle simplicity, he brings them to an utterly fresh and inventive level of cuisine. Cohen reinvents the Israeli cuisine, he challenges its tradition on a daily basis, yet he always pays homage to its roots.

BK Architects started off at the same point as Haim with an aim to represent the spirit of his kitchen. Using simplicity and honesty as primer building materials, they make use of raw and ordinary finishes. However, they are only their starting point.

Floor Plan

The open kitchen in Jaffa – Tel Aviv is the embodiment of "hospitality". Guests are invited to seat around the burning fire and watch the "show". Everything is within reach, while nothing is left behind the stage. The kitchen's stainless steel tops become a huge dining bar.

Sections

The restaurant envelope is done in the very basic materials: water, cement, aggregates and steel. Exactly as Haim's cuisine: water, flour and olive oil. The exposed concrete walls of the envelop were polished to reveal the true nature of the stone aggregates, while the concrete floor and ceiling were left untouched.

Like the culinary ingredients which come from different lands, many design elements are mixed together.

The patch work of Turkish carpets hung along the restaurant walls represents a cultural kaleidoscope. Each carpet piece has a story, an identity and a home land. They all evoke the flair of old Jaffa, a city where multi-national traditions live side by side.

The tall poplar wood shutters facing the west façade allow the sun to play a magical symphony of light and shadow upon the interior walls, a play one can always find walking the alleys of Old Jaffa. The Piet Hein Eek scrap-wood chairs and tables together with second-hand furniture pieces and outdoor light "bells" from the Czech Republic, bestow sophisticated representation of a cultural melting pot. The poured terrazzo of the alcohol bar, and the raw metal winery make a destination zone away from the lively kitchen.

Aoyama Hyotei

Completion date: 2009
Location: Tokyo, Japan
Designer: PODA, asterisk studio
Photos: Takumi Ota
Area: 216m²

Japanese restaurant "Aoyama Hyotei" is located on the first basement floor of a multi-tenant building along Aoyama Dori, the main street running across one of the most sophisticated shopping and business hubs in Tokyo.

1. Entrance
2. Entrance hall
3. Cloak
4. Bar
5. Open kitchen
6. Counter seating
7. Bench
8. Gingko objet
9. Private room
10. Washing room
11. Lavatory

Floor Plan

The restaurant features a long white counter winding around a stainless steel kitchen, and two rows of private rooms behind the walls finished with metallic brown tiles. The former countertop made of white synthetic stone shows the elegant colour of the traditional earthenware to advantage. Enjoying the dynamic cooking performed over a charcoal fire and steaming pots, the diners will be intimate spectators to share a long white dish.

Private rooms are mainly prepared for the stylish neighbours and celebrities who host a business reception or a private banquet. The ceiling of a private room painted in gold is formed in two house forms crossing. A row of four private rooms can also be used as a continuous party room, while the partitions between the rooms are stored inside the closets.

A passage between a counter and private rooms, whose ceiling is the highest, represents an open air garden alley to invite guests into tea houses. An illuminated object made of reinforced paper is raised besides the entrance hall, which is resulted from the abstraction of the stunning rows of ginkgo trees nearby. The illumination is programmed to change its colour automatically, and delight the eyes of the guests. Ginkgo leaves turning gold yellow blown from the outside, shining proudly on the sprinkled garden alley, are represented with scattered sheets of gold foils on the dark mortar floor, sealed with seamless shiny resin. The abstraction of each seasonable element is valuable not only to make dishes lively, but to take their mind off of the fact that they are dining in the basement.

Esquire

Completion date: 2011
Location: Brisbane, Australia
Designer: HASSELL
Photos: Roger D'Souza
Area: 425m²

This project was conceived and delivered through the close collaboration of architecture and interior design disciplines. An art curator was also engaged in the design process and remains responsible for the seasonal rotation of artworks. HASSELL worked very closely with the restaurant owners throughout the project to achieve a very high standard of materiality and workmanship for cost that was within their budget. The design also pursues a sustainability agenda of building well and building once through robust design and natural, durable materials that will not need to be replaced due to functional or visual decay over the life of the restaurant's operation, which is at least 10 years.

Esquire's interior design of a series of spatially diverse and connected rooms offers an experience for everyone to enjoy.

Transformed from a large commercial space into a series of intimate dining areas, guests can stop in for lunch, take pleasure in the restaurant's fine dining menu or enjoy a drink at the bar.

1. Arrival
2. Casual bar dining
3. Casual dining
4. Bar
5. Sommelier
6. Dishwashing
7. Fine dining
8. External terrace
9. Lounge
10. Fine dining kitchen
11. Semi private dining
12. Product display
13. Cloak
14. Office
15. Liquor store
16. Store
17. Back of house kitchen
18. Female bathroom
19. Male bathroom

Floor Plan

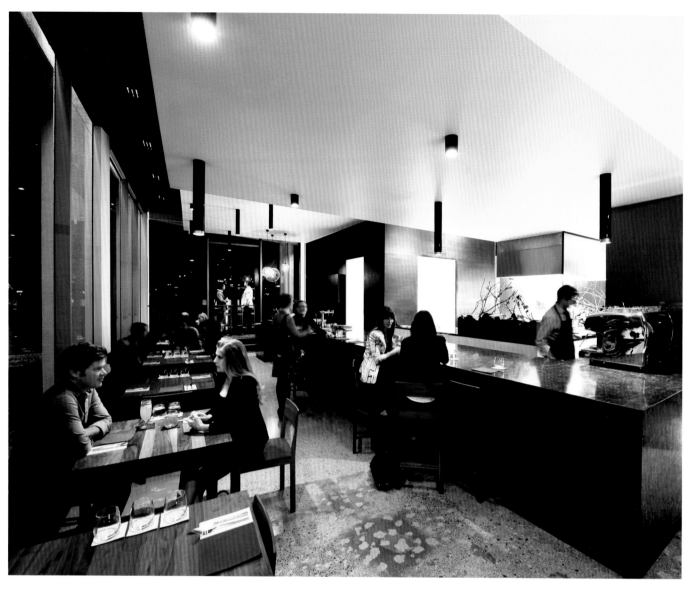

Striking a careful balance between loft and luxury, ceiling-high windows elegantly frame Brisbane's Story Bridge, while the open plan kitchens put diners in direct contact with the chefs as they prepare and plate each dish.

Burnished metal dry bar with modesty panel

Recycled timber wall with bronze glazing over

Mosaic tiled finish to dishwashing area

Stone clad columns with concealed pelmet lighting and paint finish at high level

Stone clad bar at table height

Through to lounge

Feature paint finish behind planting

Copper clad box with uplighting, hanging planters and bronze mirror cavity sliding wall

View across casual dining towards bar

Through to amenities

Woven mesh display cupboard

Upholstered banquet seat, wall panelling and ceiling with concealed lighting

Copper clad box with uplighting

Meet and greet furniture

Burnished metal entry portal with existing glazing façade

View across entry and lounge towards amenities corridor

Through the design, the HASSELL team set out to complement the artistic presentation of the food by award-winning chef Ryan Squires and his business partner, Cameron Murchison. Traditional approaches have been reinterpreted into a design that emphasises natural materials and concise detailing.

The elevated private dining room features a long wall layered with heritage timber mouldings, which are washed with light and cast into deep, textural relief.

Blown glass ball lights are suspended from Esquire's ceiling, which rises and falls in accordance with each dining space to produce a subtle but tangible variation in size and ambience.

Chapter 5: Fire Prevention in Open Kitchens

According to relative statistic data, 80% of the fire in dining places originates from kitchens. As a main location for fire, the fire prevention of the kitchen is especially important.

Fire Prevention Solutions of Open Kitchens
Due to the high potential of fire in the dining place with an open kitchen, it is inappropriate to locate it in a building with fire resistance rating lower than three. It should be located in buildings with first or second rate fire resistance rating.

5.1 Fireproof Units and Partitions

No matter the dining place with an open kitchen is located in a high-rise, multi-storey or single-storey building, it should be considered as an individual fireproof unit. First of all, the relevant components' of fire resistance should meet the design requirements. Secondly, the partition design of these places can refer to the requirements of entertainment places: to use partitions with fire resistance rate higher than 2.0h to separate it from other parts and to install first or second rate fireproof gate with thermal insulation. The area of each unit varies according to different building, storey and location and should conform to relevant rules and requirements. If the kitchen and dining area is separated by non-loading glass partition, the glass partition's fire resistance rate should achieve first rate.

5.2 Safe Evacuation

The place where open fire is used should locate near the exterior wall and try to keep away from evacuation route and exit. The kitchen and dining area should possess respective evacuation exit. At least two exits should be set near the open kitchen or the kitchen is connected to dining area with evacuation route. On the premise of at least two exits in dining area, the exits should be located far from open fire and in different directions. The technical specifications of evacuation distance can refer to those of other public spaces and be improveed according to needs.

5.3 Liquefied Petroleum Gas Pot Storage

The places where liquefied petroleum gas pots are used should set a separate pot storage, which should not be located in the middle of a storey or middle storey. The doors and windows of the storage should open outwards, never to the kitchen or inwards. The storage should have necessary explosion-proof pressure relief surface, which is kept away from public gathering place and main circulation. The storage should include an inflammable gas detector which connects to a 24h duty room. All the electrical equipment should be explosion-proof. It is prohibited to use liquefied petroleum gas pots in high-rise civil buildings, public entertainment places and underground spaces.

5.4 Firefighting Equipment

Because the decoration of dining place typically builds on existing building and the fireproof partitions exceed existing design requirements, it is necessary to enhance safety through the installation of firefighting equipment in interior design. The configuration of firefighting equipment can refer to those required in entertainment places, including automatic fire alarm system, sprinkler system, smoke control and exhaust system, kitchen fire extinguishing equipment, evacuation signs and emergency lighting.

5.4.1 Automatic Fire Alarm System
·The selection of detector. The places where pipelined gas, natural gas, gas meter and liquefied petroleum gas are used should select inflammable gas detector; the kitchen should select thermal detector; the dining area should select smoke detector. The places equipped with interactive devices and automatic fire extinguishing system should use the combination mode of smoke detector, thermal detector and inflammable gas detector.
·System interaction function. The alarm signal of detector is feedback to the control centre, and leads to shut off the emergency automatic stop valve of gas pipeline, to activate accident exhaust system, mechanical

smoke control and exhaust system, kitchen self-extinguishing devices, sprinkler system and emergency broadcasting system and to shut down non-fire power, access control system and normally open gate.

·Simple alarm system. For the smaller place inside a building without an alarm system, single point automatic fire alarm is an option. For example, a free standing inflammable detector can be activated to shut off gas pipeline valve and to open kitchen firefighting equipment or accident exhaust.

5.4.2 Automatic Fire Extinguishing System

For the building with a sprinkler system, the interior should be protected. The building without a sprinkler system should install simple fire-sprinkling system with quick response sprinkler heads. Automatic fire extinguishing devices should be installed in exhaust hood and cooking parts.

5.4.3 Smoke Exhaust System

The smoke exhaust of open kitchen should be separated from others. When natural smoke extraction is used, the window area should be maximised. In other words, the window area should not be less than 5% of the unit's area. When natural smoke extraction is not possible, a mechanic exhaust system should be installed. When in charge of one unit, the smoke exhaust rate should achieve $60m^3/h$; when in charge of two or more units, the rate should not be less than $120m^3/h$. No matter how large the open kitchen is, the connections with other parts should install smoke curtain.

5.4.4 Kitchen Firefighting Equipment

According to relevant provisions, it is recommended to install self-extinguishing equipment in fume exhaust cover and cooking area. The kitchen could also be equipped with portable kitchen extinguishers and fire blankets.

5.4.5 Mechanical Air Supply and Exhaust System

A free standing mechanical air supply and exhaust system should be installed in the kitchen. In normal working condition, the air change rate should not be less than 6 per hour. In accident condition, the air change rate should not be less than 12 per hour.

5.4.6 Evacuation Signs and Emergency Lighting
Smaller places could conform to existing design standards. However, large places such as large food court with complicated interior layout should add continuous lighting evacuation signs on evacuation walk and main evacuation route besides business areas, evacuation ways and exits.

The emergency lighting in business area, evacuation walk and stairs could apply unified illuminance. For instance, the minimum ground illuminance of the lights in the staircase should achieve 5.0 lx with appropriate spacing.

Index

AkarStudios
Add: Santa Monica,USA
Web: www.akarstudios.com

Alon Baranowitz and Irene Kronenberg
Add: Tel Aviv, Israel
Web: www.bkarc.com

Arch. Camilla Lapucci & Lapo Bianchi Luci The Studio CL
Add: Italy

asterisk studio
Add: San Francisco, USA
Web: www.studioasterisk.com

Cetra Ruddy
Add: New York, USA
Web: www.cetraruddy.com

Cherem Serrano
Add: Distrito Federal, México
Web: www.cheremarquitectos.com

Chiho&Partners
Add: Seoul, Korea
Web: www.chihop.com

Concrete Architectural Associates
Add: Amsterdam, The Netherlands
Web: www.concreteamsterdam.nl

D/Dock
Add: Amsterdam, The Netherlands
Web: www.ddock.nl

DOYLE COLLECTION CO.,LTD.
Add: Tokyo, Japan
Web: www.doylecollection.jp

Gilles & Boissier
Add: Paris, France
Web: www.gillesetboissier.com

HASSELL
Add: Austrialia
Web: www.hassellstudio.com

João Tiago Aguiar
Add: Lisbon, Spain
Web: www.joaotiagoaguiar.com

Josep Ferrando
Add: Barcelona, Spain
Web: www.josepferrando.com

k-studio
Add: Athens, Greece
Web: www.k-studio.gr

Landini Associates Pty Ltd
Add: Sydney, Australia
Web: www.landiniassociates.com

Maura
Web: www.mauradesign.com

Minas Kosmidis
Web: www.minaskosmidis.com

Stephen Williams Associates
Add: Hamburg, Germany
Web: www.stephenwilliams.com

Super Potato
Add: Tokyo, Japan
Web: www.superpotato.jp

Waraphan Watanakaroon
Add: Bangkok, Thailand
Web: www.slideshare.net

© 2014 by Design Media Publishing Limited
This edition published in May 2014

Design Media Publishing Limited
20/F Manulife Tower
169 Electric Rd, North Point
Hong Kong
Tel: 00852-28672587
Fax: 00852-25050411
E-mail: suisusie@gmail.com
www.designmediahk.com

Editing: Laura Vulto
Proofreading: Catherine Chang
Design/Layout: Pauline He

ISBN 978-988-12969-4-8

Printed in China